beauty SECRETS

DR. DEBORAH NEWMAN & RACHEL NEWMAN

Tyndale House Publishers, Inc., Carol Stream, Illinois

A Focus on the Family book published by
Tyndale House Publishers, Inc., Carol Stream, Illinois 60188

TYNDALE and Tyndale's quill logo are registered trademarks of Tyndale House
Publishers, Inc.

All Scripture quotations, unless otherwise indicated, are taken from the *Holy Bible, New
International Version*®. NIV®. Copyright © 1973, 1978, 1984 by International Bible
Society. Used by permission of Zondervan Publishing House. All rights reserved. Scrip-
ture quotations marked (MSG) are taken from *The Message* (paraphrase). Copyright © by
Eugene H. Peterson 1993, 1994, 1995. Used by permission of NavPress Publishing
Group.

People's names and certain details of their stories have been changed to protect the
privacy of the individuals involved.

Editor: Kathy Davis
Cover design by Jennifer Ghionzoli
Cover photograph © by Imagemore Co., Ltd./Getty Images. All rights reserved.
Spine photograph © by Photos.com. All rights reserved.

Library of Congress Cataloging-in-Publication Data
Newman, Deborah.
  Beauty secrets : tips for teens from the Ultimate Makeover Artist / Deborah Newman
and Rachel Newman.
    p. cm.
  ISBN-13: 978-1-58997-440-1
  ISBN-10: 1-58997-440-9
  1. Teenage girls—Religious life. 2. Body image in adolescence—Religious
aspects—Christianity. 3. Body image in women—Religious aspects—Christianity.
4. Self-acceptance in adolescence. 5. Self-acceptance in women—Religious aspects—
Christianity. I. Newman, Rachel, 1987- II. Title.
  BV4551.3.N49 2007
  248.8'33—dc22

                                            2006033413

Printed in the United States of America
1 2 3 4 5 6 7 8 9 /13 12 11 10 09 08 07

Contents

Foreword

The Bible was way ahead of us in exposing the "beauty myth" for what it is! The next time you are looking in the mirror, picture God looking over your shoulder. Here's what He has to say about you:

You Are Beautiful—You grew up and became a beautiful jewel (Ezekiel 16:7).

You Are Treasured—The Lord your God has chosen you to be His own special treasure (Deuteronomy 7:6).

You Are Honored—You are precious to God, you are honored, and He loves you (Isaiah 43:4).

You Are One Of A Kind—Before God formed you in your mother's womb He knew you. Before you were born, He set you apart (Jeremiah 1:5).

You Are Loved—He loves us with an unfailing love (Psalm 117:2).

I'm praying you will use this book you're holding as the road map it is to *real* beauty in God!

Rebecca St. James,
Christian recording artist and best-selling author

Introduction

I'm Dr. Deborah Newman, and for 18 years as a Christian counselor I helped young girls and women struggling with body image issues. A few years ago I wrote a book about body image for women, but I recognized that body image issues start early in life. That's why I asked my daughter, Rachel, to help me write a book for teens.

I remember talking to Rachel several years ago about some of the ways I helped her develop a healthy body image. Her response was, "Well, it's not that I like everything about my body; it's just that I don't care." I was so happy to hear that. She knows she isn't perfect by the world's standards, but she is free from hating her body so much that it disrupts her life.

That's the feeling I want you to have too. I want you to feel comfortable being just who you are. I'm eager to share some timeless beauty secrets that will help you be at peace with your body.

How can you really like yourself in a culture that has such unrealistic standards for the appearance of girls? When the beautiful people aren't beautiful enough without surgery and expensive beauty treatments, what hope is there for the rest of us? What is the secret to feeling beautiful in this kind of reality?

Neither one of us would say that it is easy, but we both know the secret and we want to share it with you. We meet girls every day who don't know the secret to true beauty. We've witnessed the tragedy of girls who get caught up in a beauty that promises to deliver, but in the end never does. We want to expose the myths and reveal the secret that you may have known all along in your head, but need to really believe in your heart.

I (Rachel) have watched my friends destroy themselves trying to be something they feel they need to be. I want each girl to find out who she is and replace wrong thoughts with the truth of God. I also want girls to encourage one another to grow into the beautiful women God created them to be.

I now recognize that my mom has been teaching me how to accept my body since I was a young girl. I think it really worked. I don't believe, as some of my friends do, that I have to have a perfect body, and I definitely don't want to hurt my body in the process of trying to be beautiful.

Now we want to show you some beauty secrets from the Bible that have helped us. We pray these secrets will show you the truth about how beautiful you really are.

—DEBORAH AND RACHEL NEWMAN

CHAPTER ONE

Pursuing Airbrushed Dreams

Paige has a photo shoot on Wednesday afternoon. It's a catalog shoot for the new season's bathing suits. She knows what is expected of her. At the ripe age of 15, she's learned the tricks of the trade. She can hold her abdomen in, creating the hollow look they want, while she appears to be completely relaxed on a beach somewhere. In an effort to make sure the client will be happy with her, she will not eat for three days and she'll stop drinking anything the night before—even water.

Paige did that for the last photo shoot, and whether it made her thinner or not, now she is afraid not to keep up her ritual. She knows that sometimes even one ounce of fat can mean the end of her modeling career. She has witnessed her friends being cut from jobs because they looked too heavy (in the opinion of the directors or photographers). Catalog modeling isn't very prestigious, but it does pay well and hopefully will lead to that big break Paige is dreaming of.

Even with all the work Paige puts into being thin, she won't be surprised if they airbrush her pictures. No one likes the mole on her upper shoulder; she's trying to save enough money to have it removed.

Before she became a model, Paige used to think she was beautiful. Everyone told her she was. Now she feels ugly and has become acutely aware of every body flaw. She plans to make enough money to fix everything she thinks is wrong with her body, which will involve breast implants (when she can talk her mom into letting her get them), working out at the gym with a personal trainer, and a little plastic surgery to make her nose perfectly symmetrical.

Paige is slowly giving in to eating-disorder behaviors that will soon take over her life and health. She's a truly beautiful creation of God whose pursuit of worldly beauty has destroyed her sense of dignity and worth. What Paige doesn't realize yet is that she is pursuing an airbrushed dream. The body she thinks she needs to attain to make it in the modeling world doesn't even exist in reality. (We'll talk more about that later.)

It seems kind of self-centered to admit, but if we are really honest, we all want to know that we are beautiful. The truth is that we are. No matter how beautiful you are, though, you will always feel that you need to be more beautiful if you're measuring yourself by the world's standards. Like Paige, you too will fall into the trap of pursuing airbrushed dreams of a perfect body that can't possibly exist in the real world.

We are each fearfully and wonderfully made (Psalm 139:14). That's how God wants us to see ourselves. But we won't get that message from listening to our culture. We won't get that message into our heads and hearts unless we listen to what God has to say. So where can you find His wisdom? You'll need to open the Bible in order to listen to His voice and receive His healing. That's what this study is about. In fact, we encourage you to write down or journal your feelings as part of the study. You can get a beautiful bound journal, or use a spiral notebook. It's up to you. But putting your feelings and thoughts on paper will be very revealing—especially when you go back to reread your journal at the end of the study.

We both know firsthand how frustrating pursuing the perfect body can be. I (Rachel) have grown up in a society where your outward appearance defines you. The images that constantly surround me portray girls who have been electronically altered and airbrushed so they don't even look like themselves. I have watched my friends and even myself strive to imitate these illusions in hopes of finding fulfillment. However, true purpose and satisfaction comes only in discovering God's truth. I want to share with everyone the love I have accepted from God in order to help each one of you lead lives pleasing to Him.

TEENS AREN'T ALONE

Moms battle this problem too. Your mom may be a source of pressure for you to have a perfect body. Without realizing it, she may be sabotaging your ability to fully accept yourself. As a counselor dealing with eating disorders every day, I (Debi) have tried to be extra cautious with Rachel. Even so, she has told me about things I've said that made her feel bad.

As I've dealt with teens and women as they've worked on their body-image issues, I've discovered that the only lasting cure for negative body image is spiritual. I've talked with women and girls who've suffered from eating disorders, depression, and relationship breakdowns all because they disliked how they looked. I've seen them trapped in a way of thinking that kept them in a prison of self-hatred. In their minds, there was no way out. The good news is there is a way to break out of that kind of prison; it happens through a spiritual transformation.

Are you ready to discover that you are beautiful? Think of one thing you like about yourself. It could be your eyes, your smile, your hair, even your feet. Think of that part of you, acknowledge that God made that part of you, and receive it as His gift to you. Say aloud or in your head, "I am beautiful and wonderfully made. I really like my _____ (eyes, feet, hair, etc.)." We're hoping that before long you will think positively about *every part* of yourself.

Maybe you have been so wounded by what others have said about your looks that you honestly can't find anything you think is pretty. Hopefully, with the help of your friends and this book, you will come to see your true beauty. Don't feel like an outcast. It is okay if you need some extra encouragement and someone to talk to on a deeper level about this subject. Don't be afraid to ask for the help and affirmation you may need right now.

A SUBTLE INFLUENCE

One way a lot of us lose touch with our true beauty is through the subtle influence of the media on our psyches (the center of what you think about yourself consciously or subconsciously). Each year the statistics paint a grimmer picture. Your mothers may have been influenced by the media's focus on thinness, but you are growing up in a whole new world. You are living in a culture, and maybe even in a family, that brands your body as flawed, even if you are a healthy weight and are fit. Girls in your generation will literally spend hundreds of dollars to get rid of blemishes! You live in a culture where people believe it makes perfect sense for parents to give their daughters breast implants as high-school graduation presents.

You might not realize how much you and others are influenced by the media, but you are—in dramatic ways. Picture this: You are snuggled up on the couch with your entire body feeling deliriously restful. You are completely relaxed in your most comfy pajamas, and you can see the television without straining. Your favorite show is on. Your plan is to just veg out for the next hour. You just ate, so you aren't hungry. You are where you want to be, doing just what you want to be doing. Nothing can budge you. Not even your ringing cell phone causes you to stir.

Now suppose a commercial for ice cream comes on. Suddenly, you are willing to rip yourself away from your oasis of coziness to get some ice cream. Now you can no longer enjoy your show or your contented position on the couch. Before you saw the commercial you were happy; afterward, you are preoccupied with your need for ice cream. That's the subtle influence of the media.

It has been proven that the media play a big role in making you feel that your body is flawed. When was the last time you saw a commercial or read an ad that said, "You are absolutely beautiful just the way you are. There is nothing our product can do to enhance your natural beauty"?

Dr. Margo Maine calls advertising "guerrilla warfare." In her research she has discovered that "97 percent of print ads portray women in powerless positions, as victims, sex objects, or other female stereotypes. Women are objectified and trivialized, as evident by print ads featuring a woman's full body, although often headless, but only the upper body of a man. Females are also more likely to be displayed lying down or bending over, while males stand erect."[1]

Have you ever noticed the difference Dr. Maine is talking about in the way males and females are presented? What subtle message does this difference portray to girls?

If you think models are looking thinner and thinner, you're right. They usually have eating disorders and stand in just the right positions with just the right lighting to make them look impossibly thin. However, they are still airbrushed to look "good enough." What you need to realize is that you may be in pursuit of a body that doesn't exist in reality. Even Julia Roberts, an actress famous for

Scary Statistics

- 42 percent of first- through third-grade girls want to be thinner.
- 81 percent of 10 year olds are afraid of being fat.
- 51 percent of 9- and 10-year-old girls feel better about themselves if they are on a diet.
- Without treatment, up to 20 percent of people with serious eating disorders die. With treatment, that number falls to 2 to 3 percent.
- About 50 percent of people who have been anorexic develop bulimia or bulimic patterns.[2]

her beauty, has used a body double. Most body doubles have been surgically altered to get closer to the look that Hollywood and the media consider perfect.

Not only do the media send you the message that you can and should reach for this "ideal" body for yourself, they also ignore all the other wonderful qualities girls possess. By reducing girls to what they wear, how they diet, what makeup they use, or how they smell, the message comes across that nothing else about you is important enough to feature in their magazines. They are saying that nobody really cares if you are generous, smart, kind, loyal, or friendly. To be acceptable, you need to be pretty, thin, and popular.

How have the media undermined you and kept you from accepting the brilliant, wonderful, beautiful girl you are? What are you going to do about it? Knowledge is power, and we believe it's time you think about the reality of the media and their impact on the psyches of young girls and teens.

Go over to the mirror right now and consider from head to toe how much the media, certain celebrities, current fashions, or sales clerks have influenced you to buy the clothes or products that you are wearing or have used today. Make a list of all those you can think of.

When I (Rachel) look at myself in the mirror, the first thing I notice is the way I wear my hair. My hair is long and my bangs are pushed to the side. I guess I would say that the decision to wear my hair this way is the combined influence of some stars and celebrities who wear their hair this way. The clothes I wear are cute things I put together based on what I see in magazines. Sometimes I think I "need" a tan. I guess this comes from society and friends.

Don't Think You Haven't Noticed

Even if you are the kind of girl who doesn't care what the media or others say, if you're living in the twenty-first century, you are hearing these messages.

This week try to notice how many times you are told that something about yourself is slightly flawed but can be easily remedied with a particular product. You gain power over these messages when you become aware of them, make a decision to reject them, and replace those messages with what God says about you and your beauty.

Estimate the number of times this week you were alerted to something about your body that "needs" fixing.

Don't Get Us Wrong

We're not claiming that advertising is ultimately evil. We are saying that advertisers aren't focused on your total well-being; they are focused on getting you to buy their products so they can make money. If they have to tell you that something is terribly wrong with you to get you to spend money, that's okay with them.

We want to commend Unilever, the company that makes Dove products, for the bold stand they are taking in their advertising

Quiz

Why is your hair styled the way it is?

Who influenced the type of clothes you are wearing today?

What kind of shampoo do you use?

What perfume do you wear?

efforts. They are taking a whole new approach to interest women in their products. Rather than tell us what is wrong with us, they focus on showing us how to make what we have even better. That's great. But we can't wait for the rest of the advertising world to catch on to the same wisdom.

It's as if Romans 12:2 was written in a media generation. God tells us to be "transformed by the renewing of your mind." *The Message* says it this way:

> Don't become so well-adjusted to your culture that you fit into
> it without even thinking. Instead, fix your attention on God.
> You'll be changed from the inside out. Readily recognize
> what he wants from you, and quickly respond to it. Unlike
> the culture around you, always dragging you down to its level
> of immaturity, God brings the best out of you, develops well-
> formed maturity in you.

Look this verse up in your favorite translation and write it down in your journal. This verse is the key to knowing that you are beautiful. Negative messages get into your mind. They tell you what is wrong with the way you look. When you recognize these false messages, you gain power over the impact they have on your life and your mind is transformed.

Exposing Beauty Myths

Because God created females uniquely for relationships, a lot of the focus we put on trying to be beautiful is about getting people to like us, to approve of us, and to acknowledge that we are valuable. We've found some common lies that girls believe about beauty. Read those common beauty myths below. As you read, think about whether you or your friends have bought in to any of them. Why aren't they true?

*Beauty Myth 1: If I change something about my body,
I will finally like myself.*
I (Debi) can't tell you how many girls and women ended up in my counseling office after they tried but failed to change their bodies by losing weight and getting cosmetic surgery! In fact, most anorexics and bulimics I dealt with began their eating disorders in an attempt to lose just five to 10 pounds, not hundreds of pounds! They ended up with a compulsive addiction that they felt powerless to change.

If you don't like yourself, losing weight, getting breast implants, or having a nose job isn't going to change that. Liking yourself happens in your mind, soul, and spirit.

Chesna grew up with an alcoholic mom. Her parents were divorced and couldn't get along, so she rarely saw her dad after she was three years old. Her mom was too drunk to teach her how to take care of herself. Chesna was always teased about the "rat's nest" in her hair. By the time she was 10, she was overweight, covered in freckles, and had no idea how to manage her frizzy hair.

Chesna felt ugly, but that wasn't the biggest problem in her life. Being responsible for raising herself while hiding the fact that her mom was an unfit parent was a daily struggle. After her dad remarried, his new wife encouraged him to get involved in Chesna's life again. They discovered the desperate conditions she lived in, and when she was 12, her dad and his new wife took Chesna into their home.

Judy, Chesna's stepmom, taught Chesna how to straighten her

hair and make it curl in the current style. She started eating healthy meals, and that, combined with an adolescent growth spurt, helped her slim down over the summer. Almost overnight, Chesna became the pretty girl in her new school. If there ever was a real "ugly duckling turns into a swan" story, she lived it. The problem was, no matter how much positive attention Chesna received about her looks, she couldn't stop feeling like that fat, neglected little girl inside.

How you look on the outside has little to do with whether you feel good about yourself on the inside. Studies show that beautiful people actually have a greater dislike of their looks than average-looking people.

Renew Your Mind

Healthy self-esteem comes from believing in the value God holds for you, not in the value the world (including guys) places on you. The abuse and neglect Chesna received from her alcoholic mom had damaged her view of herself. It took time and attention for Chesna to come to believe in her value and worth. She had to forgive her mom and realize that she did not cause her mom to drink. Chesna's stepmother helped her take a long journey to healing. But bad feelings about yourself do not automatically go away after you make yourself look good.

I (Rachel) know how easy it is to believe this myth. We think, *If I can just get that perfect prom dress and my hair to turn out like the picture in the magazine, I will have the time of my life.* From my years of high-school special occasions, I've discovered that it's not about what you are wearing or how your hair looks. It's about the people you are with.

Beauty Myth 2: My outward appearance is the most important thing about me.

It's totally natural for teenagers to focus on their appearance. It is part of your healthy development. But when this natural stage of development meets the youth-frenzied Western focus, it creates youth who are fixated on their appearance. This is not healthy at all. Some teens are willing to spend literally hundreds of dollars to do away with blemishes. We're not talking about teens who truly have an acne problem; normal girls with normal breakouts are getting facials and treatments at a very high cost.

Obviously parents are involved in funding these decisions. What does this kind of "help" communicate to their daughters? Sometimes well-meaning parents go along with these decisions in the hopes of raising their daughters' self-esteem, but it's not a healthy development of self-esteem and ends up increasing their insecurity. Girls get the message that appearance is all that matters about them. Do you know that in American culture, looking good rates higher on priorities than giving to the poor?

It's interesting that God sends blemishes into our lives at the developmental stage when we are most concerned with our looks. Perhaps the lesson God wants to teach us is that life will go on even when we have a horrible breakout. When you begin to believe that your appearance is all that matters, though, you don't even consider all the other qualities that make you you.

I (Debi) remember being a very skinny girl, but at age 13, skinny was in. I was also taller than average, and suddenly I started getting a lot of attention for my looks. People told me that I should be a model. I started to believe they were right and convinced my parents to let me try modeling. When the modeling school told us that I would have to pay money to be a model, I began to doubt that I was destined for stardom. I also started looking through beauty magazines and realized that there were a lot of beautiful girls in the world. I realized that I could not be the most beautiful. I decided that I would need to develop other qualities.

Too many teens today don't make the same breakthrough. They stay focused on the belief that their only value is in how they look.

Renew Your Mind

The truth is, your outward appearance is what people will first judge you by, but your personality, self-confidence, talents and abilities, and your spiritual sensitivity are all vital to who you are as well. Beauty is much deeper than how you look (1 Samuel 16:7).

It really helps you accept yourself when you stop judging other people based on their looks alone. As a therapist, I (Debi) gave girls the assignment to watch people at the mall without judging them by their appearance. Rather than thinking, *Look at that fat man,* say to yourself, *Look at that father holding his daughter's hand as they walk through the mall.* Looking for the beauty in other people helps you see the beauty in yourself. Try to think a beautiful thought about every person you have in your first-period class. Find the beauty in people, and it will help you discover the beauty in yourself.

Beauty Myth 3: Everyone can look like a movie star or fashion model if she diets enough, exercises enough, and works at it enough.
Heather's room was covered with pictures of Victoria's Secret models in their underwear. She wasn't attracted to these women; she

used these pictures to motivate herself to look like them. She believed that if she worked out hard enough and starved herself enough she could make her body look just like theirs.

If you are like Heather, we encourage you to take all your motivational pictures down. Don't brainwash yourself. Your body is your unique design. As we have already said, many of those images have been electronically altered, so the models don't even look that way in reality. In fact, if you've ever seen pictures of movie stars caught without their makeup, you know they look amazingly like average women.

People don't like to hear this, but the truth is that you are more likely to look like your blood relatives than anyone else. Don't panic if some of them are out of shape or overweight. You don't have to look exactly like them. You can get in better shape and eat more healthfully than they do. But you will have more success if you accept the body type and genetics God gave you and look the best you can with the features you have. Don't waste your time trying to copy someone else's genetics. It's not possible!

My (Rachel) mom is small boned and thin. I wanted to look like her—tall and skinny. Ironically, God gave those genes to my brother. I am bigger boned, even though my mom and I are the same height. She gave me one of her rings when I was 16, but it had to be enlarged—not because I'm fat, but because my bone structure is different.

To be as thin as my mom, I'd have to be skin and bones. I don't want to waste my life trying to be something I'm not. I've learned to be okay about the way God made me and accept that He has His reasons for making me the way I am. Perhaps one reason may be that someone reading this can relate to me and realize you don't have to be super-thin to like yourself.

Renew Your Mind

God made us in our mothers' wombs—He has reasons why we look the way we do (Psalm 139:13). I (Debi) always get a good laugh when I make this point in seminars. It's so basic and true. I have a family picture from the mid-'70s that is absolutely hideous. I asked my mom to make a copy of it because it proves this point in a dramatic way. My whole family is on the thin side and we look oh-so-funny with our knobby knees and skinny legs contrasting with our big shoes and oversized sunglasses. You'd have to see it to get the full effect.

Beauty Myth 4: Attractive people don't have any problems.

Can you think of even one of *People* magazine's most beautiful people who has a peaceful and centered life? The beautiful people of our world have problems just as normal people do. They have problems with relationships, alcohol and drugs, money, a lack of privacy, and all kinds of other things. In fact, being attractive may even create problems. One example is the Harvard librarian who claimed she was not promoted because she was too pretty.[3]

Renew Your Mind

We all have problems, and being attractive doesn't make us immune from them. Our problems stem from our sin nature, not from how we look (Romans 3:23). The culture we live in has made the scale a judge of our morality: If we can stand on the scale and it's below a certain number, then we are good; if it's over a certain number we are bad. But how much we weigh has nothing to do with whether we're good or bad. The truth is, what is really wrong with us is our broken relationship with God.

Take the focus off of other people and their problems. Renew your mind by diving into your relationship with God in order to listen to His truth and His will.

Beauty Myth 5: To be okay, I need a guy who likes me.

When Adam was created and he opened his eyes, the first thing he saw was God and the second thing he saw was the garden where he could work and make things happen. When Eve was created and she opened her eyes, the first thing she saw was God and the next thing she saw was Adam, the man she could have a relationship with. It's helpful to understand that as a girl you, like Eve, are most motivated by relationships. It's also important to become aware that you can easily be misled by relationships.

One way to be misled by relationships is by basing your identity on whether a guy likes you or not. Approval from guys is so important to young girls, teens, and young adults. It can be the focus of your thoughts day and night. You wonder why guys don't like you, or you think a guy likes you and find out later he doesn't. You pray that a guy will like you. Most girls fall into a trap of wanting male approval.

Girls idealize relationships and guys idealize bodies. The reason girls are willing to submit to painful and difficult procedures to create beauty is ultimately because they want guys to like them and pay attention to them. Really, what girl wants to live her life carrying around two hunks of silicone in her chest? After all, it's not for her own well-being. She does it so she can get the attention of a man.

Even after all the trouble a woman may go to in an effort to make herself more attractive to men by having breast implants, at least one survey questions whether it will really pay off. In a candid survey of men ranging in age between 23 and 40, the following was found:

- 86 percent prefer natural breasts to implants
- 13 percent don't care either way
- 1 percent said it depends on the age of a woman and/or prefer implants [4]

I heard one woman remark that the whole reason God put Adam to sleep when He was creating Eve was that He didn't want Adam trying to supersize her! Yet, that is exactly what is happening. Women are supersizing their breasts just to get attention from guys. Supersizing is not healthy at fast food restaurants, and it is equally damaging when we do it to our bodies.

Guys are into looks. They say stupid things about how girls look. Marie's boyfriend broke up with her because she didn't pass the "air test." According to this boy, when a girl stands with her legs together there should be air (space) between her thighs. Otherwise she is fat. That is insane! But it wasn't insane to Marie. She believed she was too fat, even though her weight and body mass index (BMI) proved that she was at a healthy weight for her body type. Most healthy girls will not have space between their thighs when they stand with their legs together!

I (Debi) know this about Marie because she came to my office suffering with anorexia. It took her two long years and thousands of dollars to recover. She fell into the trap of believing she needed her boyfriend's approval. If you have a boyfriend like that—break up with him! Take his rejection as a sign from God that he is not right for you. Look for someone who likes and accepts you the way you are.

Renew Your Mind

Teenage boys cannot give the love you are after; you have to love and respect yourself to determine what true love from a guy is all about (1 John 4:7-8). It's hard to believe now, but those great feelings you have about a certain guy are most likely not true love. When I (Debi) was your age, I thought I had found true love a time or two. But I hadn't. Real love is a commitment to an imperfect person for a lifetime. It involves good times and bad times. The only way to learn this lesson is to experience it for yourself by being open to the adventure of learning what love is. Keep in mind that girls idealize relationships to the same degree that guys idealize bodies.

Beauty Myth 6: I must compete with other girls, or at least look as good as they do.

Patty is a beautiful girl who gets lots of attention for her looks. Her best friend, Marissa, is not as cute as Patty, but when Patty found out that Marissa weighed 10 pounds less than her, she started dieting immediately. She would watch Marissa at lunch and if Marissa ate only half of a sandwich, Patty would eat a quarter of a sandwich. She kept this behavior a secret from Marissa; she didn't want her to know how insecure she felt.

There's a fine line between girl talk and competition that can get ugly. Girls bond over admiring each other's outfits. Stop and think: Who do you dress for—your girlfriends or guys? Don't you really dress to impress your girlfriends more than guys? We like our girl-friends to approve of what we wear and how we look.

Caring what your friends think and being competitive with them are two different things, though. Feeling like you have to be the cutest all the time keeps you from real intimacy. Think about the friends you hang out with. Psalm 1:1 says, "Blessed is the man who does not walk in the counsel of the wicked or stand in the way of sinners or sit in the seat of mockers." Do you hang out with friends who are in bondage to the culture? If you do, they will constantly be reinforcing the beliefs you are trying to change. Bad body image is contagious. My (Rachel) friend and I were talking about this and agree that when you are criticizing something about your body, you are indirectly criticizing your friend's same body part.

Renew Your Mind

You will always be a loser if you compare your looks and appearance with other girls', even if you think you're more attractive (2 Corinthians 10:12). God has no favorites. That is a foreign concept to us. We think we have to be better than someone else in order to feel good about ourselves. In our life with God, there is enough love and acceptance for everyone. You don't have to be a loser for me to be a winner. In God's eyes we are both winners. Healthy body image is equally contagious. When you feel good about yourself, you will automatically bring this out in others.

Beauty Myth 7: My body is who I am.

Your total beauty is packaged within your body, mind, and soul. Right after *Superman* actor Christopher Reeve was injured in a horseback riding accident and became a quadriplegic, he made this discovery: "I am not my body."[5] He couldn't believe that so many people found so much love, beauty, and value in him.

If you are going to discover your true beauty, you have to be willing to consider all the beauty you possess. True beauty is not just skin deep. You have relationships, friendships, and boyfriends because of who you are. People don't stick around because of the way you look. People are friends with you because they see something they like about you. Don't sell yourself short. Get to like yourself for who you are.

Renew Your Mind

Your body is part of you, but not completely who you are. Who you are is God's beloved daughter (1 John 3:1). Claiming that truth at the core of your being will change your life. When you can believe that God loves you beyond the boundaries of the universe, you will be on your way in your spiritual journey.

In this book we hope to help you see that it's not the image in the mirror that is the problem; it's the image in your mind. We hope to help you rediscover the joy you felt about your body around age five. A five-year-old raised in a healthy home environment (without parents who are obsessively concentrating on their looks, weight, or exercise) will feel just fine running naked through a crowd of people. Why? A child doesn't think about whether her body is better than anyone else's. She's not worried about being evaluated by her peers because of the way she looks. All the child is focused on is living and exploring the world in the body she has.

We aren't suggesting that you run around naked—far from it.

But we do hope to help you retain some of the five-year-old in you and enjoy exploring the world in the body God gave you.

Rachel: The world flashes images at us telling us what we are supposed to look like. It makes us think that there is a certain model that we need to imitate. But that's not true. God loves us. We need to learn to be happy with ourselves. It's like we're in a struggle between what the world tells us we are and what God says we are. It's not easy to change your mindset from listening to the world to listening to God. However, the freedom of life in God breaks the chains of vanity and the desire for earthly approval. Give it a try.

Debi: It's perfectly okay to desire to be beautiful. But it's wrong when your personal beauty is your whole focus in life or you are judging your beauty by the world's standards. You are not the most beautiful by the world's standards (nobody is). Discover what is most beautiful about you and start enhancing that part of yourself and accepting the rest.

Listen to God's voice by reading His Word. The Bible says that there is no condemnation toward you (Romans 8:1). Think about the fact that it was God who made you. Consider these thoughts by George MacDonald: "I would rather be what God chose to make me than the most glorious creature that I could think of; for to have been thought about, born in God's thought, and then made by God, is the dearest, grandest and most precious thing in all thinking."[6]

WEEKLY CHALLENGE

Every morning after you get dressed, focus on the part of you that you like best, whether that's your eyes, your hair, or whatever. Then say, "I thank You, God, because I am fearfully and wonderfully made and I thank You for _____ (that part you like)." Let the last message you say to yourself in front of the mirror be something positive and notice how it affects your week. In what ways are you more confident? In what ways do you care a little less that you don't have the body of a cover girl? In what ways do you like yourself just a little bit more? Are you really daring to claim your true beauty?

JUST BETWEEN GIRLS

1. How are your clothes, your haircut, your perfume, and so on influenced by the media?
2. How are you influenced to like yourself more by the media?
3. How are you influenced to dislike yourself by the media?

Airbrushed Dreams Quiz

T/F   If store mannequins were real, they would be too thin to have babies.

T/F   If Barbie was a real woman, she would have to walk on all fours to support her body.

T/F   Ninety-eight percent of women are larger than the average model.

T/F   There are eight supermodels and three billion regular women.

T/F   A size six today is equal to a size 12 ten years ago.

*These are all true!

4. Read Romans 12:1-2. Discuss the beauty myths and talk about any of them you've been believing.

5. Go around the room and name the physical quality (appearance) that you admire most about the girl to your right.

6. Go around the room and name the character quality that you admire most about the girl to your right.

7. Make a decision to focus on your best physical qualities each day. Listen for media messages that tell you that you aren't good enough or are defective in some way and answer them with Psalm 139:14: "God says I am fearfully and wonderfully made." End the group time by saying out loud one at a time, "I praise You, God, because I am fearfully and wonderfully made, and I like the way You made my _____ (physical quality you like about yourself)".
Note: You can use this body part for your Weekly Challenge exercise.

CHAPTER TWO

What You Say about Your Body Can Hurt You

 In Christina Aguilera's song "Beautiful," she sings, "I am beautiful, no matter what they say, words can't bring me down." Wouldn't that be great if it were true? The truth is, what "they say" does matter, and it certainly has the power to bring you down if you let it. To get back up, you've got to recognize how and why words have power to bring you down.

Words have deeply wounded Paige, the 15-year-old model. Paige has received attention for her looks for as long as she can remember. A blonde-haired, blue-eyed beauty who matured early, if she had an "ugly stage" no one close to her can remember it. Paige's mom tried to downplay the attention Paige received for her looks, in part because her younger sister, Katie, wasn't as striking as Paige. She also didn't want Paige to become vain.

Paige started modeling at nine when her mom's friend, who owned a children's boutique, asked if *both* girls would take part in a special layout for a mailer. Paige modeled the teenage clothes in the store. It was all so innocent, and her mom used the paycheck to begin a savings account in each girl's name. By 13, Paige was being asked more frequently to model for both adult and teen clothes. Her parents were dreaming of college tuition money, while Paige was dreaming of someday being on the cover of a magazine.

Her mom thought she was protecting her by being very practical and having strong boundaries around her career. She refused to let Paige go to Europe and live with other teens where there was steady work and more opportunities to get noticed. She wouldn't allow her to miss school for modeling and constantly reminded her that she was doing this to pay for future college tuition. Paige's mom thought she had succeeded in protecting her daughter from the dangers of modeling.

The greatest crimes against Paige's dignity and worth went mostly undetected by Paige's mom. The death blows came in subtle conversations at the lunch table. "Do you know how many calories are in that avocado?" "I never eat the week of bathing suit shoots." Then there were the not-so-subtle requests from the photographers: "Put your arm there to cover up that mole." "Suck it in now, a little more." But by far the worst words were spoken in conversations she wasn't meant to hear. Paige heard her agent speaking to a client over the phone: "I know her breasts are small. I just haven't had the right signals from her mom to talk about that yet. Yes, her mole will be removed in the future, but we've had great results on her touch-ups."

It's hard enough being a normal girl in a normal world. How

would you like to work in a job where other people were constantly commenting about your body? Even outside the modeling field, though, people are continually criticizing your body. Their words do affect you.

In my (Debi) experience as a Christian counselor I've discovered that while the media regularly reinforce the negative beliefs you have about your body, in most cases the real damage stems from statements made by significant people in your life.

I could give you example after example of teenagers who can tell you the exact words that made them hate their bodies and sent them on their tailspin into depression, eating disorders, or cutting. I have two standard questions I ask in counseling that help reveal the underlying causes of people's body hate:

1) What is it that you like least about your body?

2) When do you first remember hating that part of yourself?

Most often the answer to question number two is a comment or words spoken by someone significant in their lives about the part of their body they say they hate most. The power of words is huge and God knows it. Proverbs 18:21 describes it this way: "The tongue has the power of life and death."

You need to think about what death words have been spoken about your body so you can receive the power to confront them and heal from them. Most of us have been called a name or heard a negative comment about a body feature by another person.

But just because death words are spoken to us doesn't mean that we have to remain victims of them the rest of our lives. If we open our ears and hearts to the reality of what is going on, we will gain power to overcome them. Media messages and death words spoken by others have power only when you let them float around inside your soul, subtly influencing how you think about yourself. When you face them and tell yourself the truth instead, you have found the key that releases you from the prison of body hate.

Be sure you do the Weekly Focus exercise this week. You may want to turn to page 43 right now and complete it before you finish this chapter. It will help you apply what you just read.

Now it's time for you to answer those two questions, if you haven't already:

1) What is the part of your body that you like least?

2) When did you first starting hating that part of yourself?

Messages Girls Have Received

"Wart Girl."—a name Carly was called on the playground in first grade

"It wouldn't hurt for you to lose 10 pounds."—a comment made by Jen's mom while Jen tried on dresses for homecoming

"Your dance costume was a special order, so it didn't come with the others."—explained to Lucy, who was the largest in her class

"Look at your pudge."—made by a girlfriend

"Your arm fat jiggles."—made by a boyfriend

"You are so short."

"You are too tall."

"You have a big butt."

"You have some freaky nostrils."

Ginny hated her weight. Her mother made the "helpful" comment to her, "You know the teenage years are the thinnest you will ever be, so you'd better watch what you eat." Linda hated her small breasts. She remembers the day her dad made fun of her and commented that there wasn't much there. Sharon thinks her butt is the biggest one in the world. Her dad asked her, "Sharon, have you gained a little weight?" When Sharon answered "No," he smiled and said, "I guess you can't see where it has gone," pointing to her behind.

Ally's gymnastic coach thought up a new way to keep the girls motivated. He instituted mandatory weigh-ins at Monday practices. Before Ally stepped on the scale that first Monday, she'd never had a concern about how much she weighed. When she stepped off, her coach made the comment that she needed to lose only one or two pounds. Ally threw up for the first time that night and hasn't been able to stop since.

The words that have been spoken to you about your body stay with you.

Writing this today, I (Debi) think about an encounter I had with a stranger on a tennis court involving words spoken about my body. All these years later, I can recall something that should have been totally insignificant to me, but still remains in my memory. I want to share it with you so you will better see what I mean about taking charge of your own beliefs about your body.

By far the thing I liked least about my body was my small breasts. I hated it at the time, but now I am thankful that God gave me small breasts. I believe my lack of confidence about that part of my body kept me from making some stupid sexual choices when I wasn't walking with God. But despite my small breasts, I thought I was something special because I did get a lot of attention for my looks.

One time my best friend, Brenda, and I were playing tennis. Though we were no competitors on the tennis court, we were getting exercise and laughing at each other's inabilities. Brenda and I were having a good time, so I hadn't even given the teenage boys using the court on my left a second thought.

I overheard one of the boys say to the other, "What about them?" The one closest to me said, "No, she has the wrong top." He didn't even know how to comment properly on my body. I don't think I told Brenda what he said; I just went on with my life enjoying my fun, thinking, "I am way out of his league no matter what he says." But I still remember his words.

This was a comment made several decades ago by a person I didn't know or care about. I shouldn't be able to remember a moment like that. I do, though, because in that seemingly insignificant moment words were spoken about my body that reinforced my insecurity. In my head they meant nothing, but they affected me in my psyche (where I stored all the reasons I wasn't good enough). Remembering that comment was part of the healing process I went through in coming to the freedom to love and be at peace with my body.

The words of people, usually those you love and respect such as parents, coaches, boyfriends, and friends, may have affected you deeply in the way you look at yourself. Before you can heal from the hurt their words have caused, you need to recognize that pain.

Why relive something painful? It feels like the wrong thing to do. You just want to make it go away, not think about it. But you need to remember so that you can make the conscious decision whether you want those words to be the way you form your opinion about yourself. We make inner decisions every day. I replaced what that stranger said about my body with the truth that God had a purpose in designing me the way He did.

Have you recalled some hurtful statements? If so, you need to confront them with God's truth. In her song "Beautiful," Bethany Dillon describes the cry of the heart of every girl and the transformation that is possible when we really open ourselves to God's truth. She identifies the desire that lives inside every girl to be beautiful. She reveals the self-hate when that beauty doesn't seem to get the attention she was after.

I was so unique
Now I feel skin-deep
I count on the makeup to cover it all
Crying myself to sleep, 'cause I cannot keep their attention
I thought I could be strong
But it's killing me
Does someone hear my cry?
I'm dying for new life

Then she gets it. Finally, she understands that it is God who makes her beautiful. He says that who you are is quite enough. That ends up making you beautiful and worthy of love. It's because He says you are worthy!

You make me beautiful
You make me stand in awe

You step inside my heart, and I am amazed
I love to hear You say
Who I am is quite enough
You make me worthy of love and beautiful[1]

CONFRONTING NEGATIVE WORDS
SPOKEN ABOUT YOUR BODY

We all fight the shame from negative messages about our bodies. Everything is going great until suddenly you get an emotional sensation so paralyzing that it feels as though you can't breathe; you can't look in the mirror; you can't stand the thought of who you are housed in your body.

Why does it happen? Because Satan knows that if he can keep us focused on ourselves and what we need to do to change our bodies, we will never know how really beautiful we are. He can make us sing, "I wish I were beautiful, no matter what they say." And one of the best ways he does this is to bury the negative statements that have been made about us under a layer of denial. We think it's ridiculous that we'd feel hurt just because our dads told us to stop eating so fast or we'd get fat! We tell ourselves it didn't make a difference, but that's not true, is it?

Once you identify what words are weighing you down, you need to heal from them through forgiveness. Even if you think the people weren't that significant or they are completely out of your life or they are dead, you still need to take the time to forgive.

Forgive. How do you know if you've done it? When you have forgiven your boyfriend, a stranger, your mom, your dad, or a sibling for the hurtful words spoken to you or about you, you will feel free from the aftereffects of what they did or said to you. It is really unbelievable how God can fix everything that is so messed up in this world. But He can.

You might think God tells us to forgive so the person we forgive will become a better person. But through forgiving, we benefit more. When we forgive someone for hurting us, we let go of the poison of hatred. We don't let that person have power over us by hating him or her.

Think of someone who has made a negative comment to you about your body—a stranger, a guy, a coach, a sibling, a parent. Say out loud, "God, help me forgive _____." That's your part. God does the rest. He will help you truly forgive and see the truth about who you really are. But remember that it takes a long time to forgive some things, while other things are easier to forgive. Don't be frustrated with yourself if forgiveness doesn't come easy. Keep talking to God about it.

There are three important parts of the process of forgiveness. The first is that you must be brutally honest about the feelings you have about the wrong done to you. I recommend that you write a letter of anger to the person who spoke harmful words to you. You will not send this letter; its purpose is to help you acknowledge what has been festering in your soul all these months or years. The purpose is to release the toxins and acknowledge to yourself and God that you have a wound that needs His healing power.

The second phase is to confess your own sins. How have you sinned against God, your own body, or others because you have been trying to protect yourself from this hurt, rather than healing through forgiveness? In considering the ways you have sinned against others, think about comments or words you have spoken about other people's bodies, or even ways you have behaved because you are jealous of other girls.

The last part is simply to commit to the forgiveness process. This is an invitation for God to come into your soul and, through forgiveness, clean out the damage that the wound has left inside of you.

WHAT A GIRL WANTS

Your need for love drives your craze for self-improvement. The media and rejection from others cause you to believe that when you are pretty enough and perfect enough, you will have all the love you need. It's time to look at your legitimate need for love and discover the only way you can find true, meaningful love.

Love comes from God. It might seem so far away and hard to reach. You equate love of God with the love of your grandmother— she loves you because she doesn't know any better! Nothing could be further from the truth about God. He knows you and loves you. He made you. He designed your body and created you with the unique beauty you possess. You can embrace the way He made you, and look for reasons that He chose your size and looks. How you are made reflects the purpose God has designed for your life.

I (Debi) think my design has been helpful in discovering how God wanted me to serve Him. For instance, I've never been athletic. In fact, as a college student I could only compete alongside seventh-grade girls in volleyball. Obviously I wasn't designed to use athletics to minister. Sometimes people ask me why I specialized in eating disorders. I did not choose eating disorders; they chose me. At the hospital, the eating disorder patients wanted me as their counselor. They seemed to think that since I was thin I wouldn't make them get fat. A certain degree of trust developed because of the way I looked. What can you discern about God's future plans for you by the way He made your body?

God spent time thinking through the whole package that makes you you! He never intended for us to compare our looks with each other, but to see ourselves as a reflection of His image. We all have one thing in common: We each have the image of God. He says that our bodies are the place He dwells (1 Corinthians 6:19).

We need to trust how much God loves us, including the bodies He gave us. One way to help yourself accept the love of God is to write a letter from God to you about how much He loves you and how He created you just the way you are. Here is an example of a letter. After reading it, take the time to write yourself a letter.

Dear Elly:

I love you. I remember the time I took deciding just which parents you would be born to. I love your mom's curly red hair and I thought you would look great in it. I know that you wish you had her blue eyes, but I did something unique when I gave you hazel eyes that turn green in the sunlight. You see, I have plans for your unique life. I created you in just the right way to attract the life partner I have planned for you. Other men may not see the beauty I placed in you, but one day the one I chose for you will surprise you completely.

I'm proud of what I made, but I'm also looking forward to the new body I will give you in heaven. What you are living in now is just dust, in a way. It will not last forever. It is your temporary housing while you are here on earth. But I do want you to take care of your body so that you have the time and energy to do all that I have planned for you to do on this earth. You are going to love walking with Me. I will show you how to get the most out of all your relationships. I will guide you to just the right people to help you along your journey.

I'm glad you can see how you are fearfully and wonderfully made.

Love,

Your Heavenly Father

GOD HAS HIS REASONS

Why do you think God gave you the body flaws you have? Right now I'm (Debi) thinking of two interns I knew several years ago. Both were eager to serve God. Both had a passion for sharing God's Word with others in an exciting way. They were dynamic communicators. It was more than obvious that God had given them a special gift of insight, humor, and favor with the people they met.

One of the young men was cute but had a severe acne problem that left scars all over his face. The other was very good looking from the world's standards. Girls had crushes on both of them because they were such dynamic leaders, but the good-looking intern did get a little more attention than the one with scars.

A few years later, I got a report on how they were doing. The one with acne continued to use his gifts for God's glory and was now the pastor of a dynamic and growing church. The other had gotten a girl pregnant and was painting houses while deciding whether to marry her. It was easy to think that God had blessed the good-looking one a little bit more. In reality, the acne issues may have made the other one a better servant of God. Perhaps they kept him from getting distracted from God by being overfocused on the attention he could get from girls.

Could one of your body flaws be perfectly designed by God to help you grow closer to Him and more apart from the world? That kind of thinking is really hard when you are a teenager. I (Debi) didn't begin to think this way until I was an adult, far away from so much of the pressure to look good that is in your face every day. But I want to challenge you to think about your looks like that.

Consider what God might have been thinking when He gave you that thick waist, those big feet, or that slow metabolism. Does He have something good in mind for you? God thought you up. Believe it or not, He wanted you to have that frizzy hair. He thinks it is glorious.

Ultimately, when others see our love for God, we are the most beautiful. It isn't really about our hair or bodies, although God designed them for us. Our beauty comes from showing Christ to others.

Confronting Your Belief that Teenage Boys Will Bring You the Love You Want

A lot of the hurt we carry comes from the experiences we've had with guys. We get all messed up in our feelings about boys. I (Rachel) accidentally overheard a statement made to my brother by a 13-year-old girl that really made me sad for all of us girls. I picked up the phone to make a call and heard a young girl chattering to my brother, who was also 13. She was telling him about the "love life" of one of their friends and how when a boy broke up with her, she decided to become anorexic. Hopefully the friend did not become anorexic, but it's really sad to think that anorexia seems a reasonable solution when a guy doesn't like you.

It's totally normal for you to be wondering what boys think and whether boys like you. It is totally unhealthy to think that if a boy likes you, you will like yourself better. Liking yourself has to happen inside of you. No one can ever like you enough to erase the scars of your not liking yourself.

There's one thing I (Debi) learned as a teenager. Teenage boys do not have the love you want! Being pretty doesn't get you the love you want. God is the One who has the love you want. He even wants to show you how to enjoy the love you may get from a relationship with a teenage boy. You've got to trust Him and believe that He knows what He is talking about. Among the four things just too amazing on this earth is "the way of a man with a maiden" (Proverbs 30:18-19). God delights in the special feelings you are learning about in your guy-girl relationships. You can trust Him to show you how to enjoy them most fully.

Why do you want a boyfriend? Why does a 13-year-old think she needs to be anorexic if the boy she likes doesn't like her back? What is going on inside girls? Here's the truth: Girls don't think that they are good enough on their own. Somehow, they don't feel worthy unless someone loves them. Unfortunately, it just doesn't work that way. Let's expose the facts about teenage boys.

WHAT TEENAGE BOYS CAN GIVE

Status: A fake sense of love. It makes you feel important to have someone that likes you and wants to be with you. When you have a boyfriend, it takes a little of the attention off the question of whether you are desirable or not. He's your boyfriend, so it's proof you are wanted. Part of the status comes in thinking you're better than other girls who don't have a boyfriend. It's okay to want to be wanted. You were created to be wanted. But that can be a problem when your desire to be wanted causes you to make decisions that compromise your standards.

Safety: Similar to status, but slightly different. You will have a sense of safety when you can get and keep the attention of a guy. You have an answer for friends and relatives who haven't seen you for a year when they ask, "Do you have a boyfriend?" For teens this translates, "Are you normal?" You can be safe on Valentine's Day and for other important events. You don't have to worry about being alone.

A sense of love: What drives you most to want a boyfriend is that you get a sense of being loved. In the future when you finally find real love, you will understand that teenage relationships probably weren't real love. Right now, though, it feels like a boyfriend's love is filling up that longing you have to know that somebody loves you.

WHAT TEENAGE BOYS CAN'T GIVE

As you enjoy relationships with guys in the teen years, be sure you fully understand what boyfriends are unable to give you. This way you can enjoy your relationships with guys better without giving them the place only God can fill.

True self-worth: Teenage boys cannot give true self-worth—that can come only from within you. It is something God shows you about yourself. When you are depending on a guy to give you self-worth, it is only temporary because eventually you will probably break up and your sense of self-worth will break up also. (Remember, most people don't marry a person they went with in high school.)

Purpose and meaning: We all need purpose and meaning in our lives, and trying to get them from a teenage boy is a meaningless pursuit. Making your boyfriend feel loved, making him the center of your universe, is definitely not the purpose God has given you. If a guy becomes your purpose and meaning for living, it won't be enough. You are designed for so much more than just being somebody's girlfriend.

Unconditional love: Teenage boys are incapable of unconditional love because all human love is conditional. We can't help it. We are not great at loving others above ourselves. Unconditional love comes only from God. Even your parents are not perfect at giving unconditional love.

The good news is that what boys can't give, God can. And He desperately wants to give you what you need. The best advice I (Debi) ever got as a teen was from Ecclesiastes 12:1: "Remember your Creator in the days of your youth, before the days of trouble come and the years approach when you will say, 'I find no pleasure in them.'" I started to give my focus to God and stopped trying to get guys to like me. I still liked them and enjoyed the attention they gave me, but I wasn't dependent on them in order to like myself.

What a Boy Can Give	*What a Boy Can't Give*
Status	True self-worth
Safety	Meaning and purpose
A sense of love	Unconditional love

We've looked at the fact that words can hurt. But even though they hurt, God can heal us. Are you willing to receive God's healing? That's what this book is designed to do. It is giving you God's Word, interactive experiences, and personal reflection that provide opportunities for you to be healed by God.

Rachel: We've all been hurt by something someone has said about us. It's just a fact. However, we must learn to overcome those words with the truth of God's love. I pray that God has touched your heart so that you can begin to heal. The beauty is that God's abundant love will always satisfy you.

Debi: I've been shocked in my counseling experience to realize how devastating words have been in the lives of women. I'm equally amazed at the healing force God's Word is in mending the pain. None of us is doomed to live out the legacy of statements that have been made about us. We can all find freedom. God wants to tell us who we really are. I hope you receive the power of His healing words through this study.

WEEKLY CHALLENGE

1. Write down all the names you have been called or negative statements about your body that you can remember. We know this is painful, but trust us long enough to do this exercise.

2. Cross out each one. Now, from the list below find the truth about who you are in God's opinion and write it beside each lie. Ask God to help you remember everything you need to remember.

You are God's possession—1 Peter 2:9

You were wonderfully made—Psalm 139:14

God chose you long ago—Ephesians 1:5

God created you to do good works—Ephesians 2:10

You are made in God's image—Genesis 1:27

You can call God "Daddy"—Galatians 4:6

You have been bought with Christ's blood—Ephesians 2:13

Christ loves you so much He died for you—John 3:16

You are without fault because of Christ—Colossians 1:22

You are sealed by the Holy Spirit—Ephesians 1:13

God lavishes His grace on you—Ephesians 1:7-8

You are forgiven—Colossians 3:13

You are accepted—Romans 15:7

There is no condemnation toward you—Romans 8:1

You are God's daughter—1 John 3:1

God will never leave you—Joshua 1:5

3. Tear up the sheet and throw it in the garbage as a sign of the decision you have made not to believe these statements about who you are anymore.

JUST BETWEEN GIRLS

1. On a scale of 1-10 (10 being the highest), how much do you think you are hurting from words spoken to or about you?

2. Have you ever really forgiven someone? How did it feel? How do you know when you have forgiven?

3. What can you learn about the purpose God might have for your life by the way He made you?

4. Why do you think we are so mean to each other and say negative things about our bodies and others' bodies?

5. On a scale of 1-10 (10 being the highest), how important is it to you that you have a boyfriend, and why?
6. How can God heal hurtful words from our past?
7. Have one girl stand up in front of the group. Next have each girl in the group say the name of the girl who's standing and repeat what God says about her from this list until every statement is made. (In small groups, each girl will say two or three truths.) Repeat the exercise until every girl present has stood in front of the group.

   Statements to repeat:

   _____, you are God's possession.

   _____, you were wonderfully made.

   _____, God chose you long ago.

   _____, God created you to do good works.

   _____, you are made in God's image.

   _____, you can call God "Daddy."

   _____, you have been bought with Christ's blood.

   _____, Christ loves you so much He died for you.

   _____, you are without fault because of Christ.

   _____, you are sealed by the Holy Spirit.

   _____, God lavishes His grace on you.

   _____, you are forgiven.

   _____, you are accepted.

   _____, there is no condemnation toward you.

   _____, God will never leave you.

   _____, He loves you.

   _____, and so do I.

CHAPTER THREE

How Not to Feel Fat in That

Melissa can't remember when she lost touch with who she was. She doesn't remember when she stopped being herself. She used to laugh when she found something funny. Now she laughs only when her friends are laughing. She doesn't have feelings; instead she just feels fat. Rather than feel, she constantly asks herself and others, "Do I look fat in this?"

A long time ago Melissa would share how she felt. She would give her opinion just because she had an opinion. Now she holds back and speaks only when she knows her opinion will be validated by the others. It used to bother her when her friends were cutting down someone behind her back. Now she doesn't even care if the person being talked about can hear what is said.

Melissa is in a pretty good crowd at school. She and her friends are considered popular. She feels fortunate to be accepted by such a high class of girls. It gives her a sense of relief to know that she has a group to eat lunch with, a group she can approach without being turned away.

In order to be part of this group, though, Melissa has been

forced to stop feeling and being herself. She thinks that the new girl's vintage t-shirt and skirt are kind of cute the way she put them together with her funky jewelry. But she knows she will never try it after the way her friends laughed at the girl's outfit all day.

Day by day, Melissa cuts herself off more from her feelings. Soon she is feeling only what the girls in her group are feeling. She is disgusted by the same things they are. She doesn't care about hurting people's feelings anymore. Cutting herself off from her feelings is a subtle choice that leads to numbness. When she gets in a fight with her mom, rather than feel discounted, she looks down at her stomach and just feels fat. In fact, that's all she feels now.

When Melissa lost touch with her true feelings, she was left with only the superficial, only what was outside of her. That's why today if you ask her how she feels, she'll tell you she feels fat. She's not trying to be difficult. Because she lives in a superficial world, she feels only skin deep.

You don't have to work with girls who have body-image issues for many years before you want to jump up and scream, "Fat is not a feeling!" when they tell you how they feel. And although fat really, really isn't a feeling, telling them this truth will not help. Honestly, fat feels like a feeling to them. Fat is a way to disguise your feelings. Fat is a way to numb yourself from what you truly feel about life, people, and other things you have absolutely no control over.

When girls lose touch with their feelings, they lose touch with their true selves. They develop false selves. They deny who they really are.

Alyssa puts the leftover negative feelings she has about her horrible life into her workout program. She's scared to death of throwing up. She's heard all kinds of horror stories about how girls have gotten bad teeth and heart problems from doing it. So instead of throwing up, she purges every bite of food she takes in by exercising constantly. Her parents started to worry when they noticed that her arms are the same size as her five-year-old sister's. Previously they were proud of Alyssa for being a good athlete when she was running three to four miles a day. Now they're worried that she's overdoing it.

Alyssa's parents are well-respected people in the community and at church. They provide well for Alyssa, and she always has the best. The "best" is definitely expected of her in return. She has to have the best grades, the best clothes. She has to eat right. All of this pressure to be perfect makes Alyssa feel a lot of anger toward her parents. Until recently, slamming doors, staying isolated in her room, or screaming, "I hate you, stay out of my life" were how most attempts at conversation ended in Alyssa's family. This kind of release made her feel guilty.

Then Alyssa discovered the perfect way to release her leftover, negative feelings: She could control her body. It distracts her from how much she hates her life and her parents for wanting her to be perfect. It gives her a false sense that she is being perfect so she can feel better.

Have you lost touch with your feelings? Do you slam doors, scream, or isolate yourself when you have feelings? Do you cover up your feelings by feeling fat or trying to be perfect? Your feelings are very important to discovering that you really are beautiful, so you need to be in touch with them. When you feel beautiful, you act beautiful. The 2006 *American Idol* runner-up, Katherine McPhee, describes distancing herself from her feelings by using food: "Food was my crutch; it was how I dealt with emotions and uncomfortable situations. As soon as I would feel something, I would eat over it so that I didn't have to feel anything I didn't want to."[1]

It's very important to find out why you replace your true feelings with the feeling of fat (ugly, unfit, or whatever). You need to get in touch with your real feelings and work to resolve them. Let's find out how to make friends with your feelings.

Two Ways to Deal with Emotions

Girls will deal with their emotions in one of two ways. One way is to bury them deep inside. This is what Melissa has been doing by feeling fat. The problem is that when you bury your emotions, you are burying an important part of yourself that you need to be a healthy person. Alyssa chose to express all her negative emotions first through anger at her parents and then through obsessive exercise. Neither was a good long-term option. She ended up in the hospital with anorexia.

There is a third and healthier way to deal with your feelings. You can accept feelings as part of the way God designed you to function and learn how they can help you live your life.

Managing the Highs and Lows of Emotions

When God created you as an emotional being, He did it for a reason: It was one of the ways He was making you in His image. Did you ever think about the fact that God has feelings too? He feels love. He feels anger. He feels jealousy. He also has no sin. Emotions are not sin. But how we handle our emotions can be sinful.

God doesn't have mood swings. In fact, He is slow to anger (Psalm 103:8). God teaches us how to handle our emotions so we won't hurt ourselves the way Melissa and Alyssa have. Dealing with negative emotions in a dysfunctional way is how people get started on the cycle of addiction. It's really important to a healthy life that you discover the freedom of knowing what to do when you get overwhelmed by emotions like stress, anger, hurt, shame, jealousy, and others.

Melissa and Alyssa are handling their emotions, but not in ways that bring them peace. Confronting your emotions with truth is the way to heal from negative feelings. Stuffing your feelings and changing something about your body won't fix your emotions.

Changing Your Mind about Your Feelings

Facing your feelings and training your mind to think on truth will leave you feeling beautiful just the way you are. Knowing the truth about how God made you can change your mood. This may seem hard to believe, but what harm can come from giving it a try? When you know that God designed you exactly the way you are and that He has a purpose for you, you may look at your freckles a little differently. If you believe they are unique beauty marks, you will feel more confident in how you look. If you replace the thought *Boys in elementary school called me "freckle face"* with *God gave me freckles that make me unique,* you will replace your feeling of shame with a feeling of confidence. That kind of confidence makes you more attractive.

Melissa and Alyssa have very negative feelings about their lives and their looks. It would be healthy for them both to admit their true feelings. They need to have the courage to say they hate things, they are jealous of others, and they hurt. Let's go over the steps to having healthy feelings.

Step One: Identify your feelings.

Feelings are automatic responses to what you think about your circumstances. You can't change your feelings by simply saying "I don't feel that way." However, you can *control* your feelings by changing how you *think*. Identifying your feelings leads you to discover what you are really thinking. For example, Courtney felt angry that Katie got a higher math score. Courtney may not have consciously thought that she wanted to be better than Katie because it would make her feel better about herself. It wasn't until she thought deeper about her anger that she recognized her true vanity.

Your negative feelings signal that something is wrong. All feelings are real, but not all feelings are true. For instance, you may feel ugly, disgusting, and worthless. Those are real feelings. But you are God's beloved creation, and as such, you are beautiful, appealing, and worth more than gold.

What do you feel? Often when you have negative feelings about your body, it is caused by feelings from other realities in your life that you sense no control over. You transfer those bad feelings to your body because you rationalize that you can control your body. You mistakenly think that if you can make your body look a certain way, all of your other negative feelings will go away. It never happens. Negative feelings can haunt you for years unless you learn that changing your thoughts is the only way to resolve them.

It's important for you to know it's okay to feel bad sometimes. So many addictions (including eating disorders) get started because of our "feel good" addiction. Jesus never told us that we should always be happy, but we seem to feel we have that right. We need to be okay with feeling angry, sad, hurt, lost, or anxious at times. Our feelings tune us in to what we are thinking and why we are behaving a certain way. We need to give up the notion of being happy and concentrate on discovering why we are experiencing a particular emotion.

It's totally normal to not feel good enough. We've already discussed the fact that every day you fail to measure up to others' expectations. This is the way Satan keeps you bound up in hating yourself. He never wants you to begin to see who you really are. You will go through your whole life not feeling like you measure up until you learn to identify your feelings and confront them with the truth of God's Word.

That might sound like an overly spiritual thing to do, but honestly it's the only way to break free.

Circle the words that describe what you are feeling right now.

Gorgeous	Angry	Anxious	Content	Pleased
Embarrassed	Proud	Like a loser	Whole	Vain
Hideous	Lost	Worried	Unhappy	Elated
Disappointed	Elegant	Gratified	Fearful	Hurt
Frustrated	Ashamed	Arrogant	Confident	Sad
Other _____ (You name it)				

Step Two: Identify the ways your negative feelings are harming you.
You can think of your feelings as an alarm system for your body and soul. They can be very helpful to you in drawing your attention to important stuff you might be too preoccupied to look at. Everyone has had one of those false fire alarms at school. Sometimes they can get you out of a totally boring class, but for the most part they're a nuisance. Most often, fire alarms are practice drills or a student playing a prank. Rarely do they go off because there is a real fire.

But you've got to pay attention to every fire alarm just in case it's the real thing.

Feelings function like fire alarms. Sometimes they are false, but sometimes they are real. Either way, you need to take notice of them so you can find out which is which.

Melissa circled the feeling "ashamed" from the list above. She can vaguely feel the shame in her soul when her friends are talking about people right in front of them. It just doesn't feel right. She has been working on ignoring this feeling, but if she will think about it for a minute, she can see that this negative feeling is harming her. She feels like one of those mean girls. It's making her think even less of herself than she already does. Maybe she is having that feeling of shame because God is trying to reach her. Maybe He is trying to help her see that hurting other people is no way to feel better about herself.

What a Girl Feels

- Lonely because no boys like me
- Angry that my brother won't get out of the bathroom
- Annoyed that my mom didn't wash the shirt I was planning to wear today
- Stupid because I can't understand today's math class
- Ignored by my friends
- Worried that my friend is having sex
- Hurt that my dad ignores me
- Worried that I won't get asked to prom
- Confused about what I'm going to do with my life
- Defeated because I'm working so hard at school but my grades don't show it

If Melissa will acknowledge her feelings, they might lead her to the source of her problem, which is how much she dislikes herself. She needs to confront the fact that she feels insecure and that even her efforts to fit in are hurting her. She needs to get to the root of why she feels so unacceptable.

Step Three: Decide to believe the truth.

Once you identify your feelings, you need to confront them with truth. Melissa feels like a loser and a misfit, and that's why she tries so hard to fit in. Melissa is not a misfit. She is so glad that she went to youth group the night Carrie, a 20-year-old college student, shared her testimony. Melissa could relate to everything Carrie shared.

Carrie talked about how she wasted her high-school years and her freshman year of college trying to fit in. She talked about the things she did, the parties she went to, the guys she dated, and the things she did on dates. But the thing she hated most was the way she and her friends bullied a girl in their class in high school.

The girl was different from Carrie and her friends. Her name was Mary and she was from a strict religion. She wore knee-length, out-of-date dresses every day. She had never cut her hair, and she had very bad acne. Carrie remembers the day her boyfriend, Curt, chastised her and her friends for being so mean to Mary. That felt a little bad, but most of the time it felt good to hurt Mary. Carrie saw her as a non-person. During Carrie's freshman year of college while she was home on Thanksgiving break, she found out that Mary had just committed suicide. Carrie had a nauseated feeling in the pit of her stomach when her mom blurted out the news. She didn't want to cry, like you might think she would. She connected the nauseated feeling with the thought that maybe it was her fault Mary died.

Something compelled Carrie to attend Mary's funeral. While she was there, Carrie's guilt faded to a sense of how much she related to Mary. Mary had been an obvious misfit, but she'd had feelings too. She didn't know how to please her family and the people at her high school at the same time. Her family and church values kept her from fitting in with the other kids at her school. She was a loner.

During the funeral, Carrie felt she could understand why Mary wanted to die. There was a sense of hopelessness in the whole mood of this funeral. After attending the service, Carrie felt so confused. She stopped by her church and met with her old youth minister. Carrie told her about the bad feelings she was having. She confessed that she realized she was really no different from Mary.

Her youth minister helped Carrie see what God wanted her to do with those feelings of guilt and hopelessness. He wanted her to confess her sin of bullying Mary and receive God's forgiveness. This turned Carrie's life around. She was eager to help other girls see what they were doing to each other and understand why they were doing it.

She wanted the cool girls and the girls who were not cool to find out that they both had the same feelings of insecurity deep down. Carrie explained that all girls are afraid that they are not wanted or loved. Then Carrie related how receiving God's forgiveness and His love totally changed her life. Now she is so secure in His love that she is willing to share these embarrassing truths about her past with high-school girls.

Melissa talked to Carrie after the session. Carrie promised to pray for her. God has hope for every misfit everywhere. There is no one who doesn't fit in. We are each designed perfectly to fit just the way God made us.

Step Four: Eliminate body shame and sexual shame.
Shame is the most basic negative feeling we have. Girls seem to have a lot of shame about their bodies and sexual issues. A significantly high number of girls with body image issues and eating disorders have experienced some kind of unwanted sexual encounter. Often they feel so much shame and disgust for their bodies that they punish them. If this is what has happened to you, we encourage you to tell someone you can trust. There is no way that we can give you the support and help to see yourself the right way just in this book. You need to discover the beauty of healing through giving the shame back to the person who hurt you and by learning to forgive. Talk to a spiritual leader or ask your parents about talking to a Christian counselor who can help you do this.

Part of learning to let go of negative feelings about your body is receiving God's forgiveness. If you are trapped in the pit of shame and disgrace because of sexual experiences you've had, God invites you to be cleansed. I love the way God describes what actually happens when He forgives us. He makes us sparkling clean. He literally cleanses us from the stain of sin. We are made new through His cleansing blood! You don't have to feel defiled by sexual shame and sin. You can be clean (1 John 1:9). If shame is a feeling that you identify with strongly, please talk to someone such as a counselor or mentor about this. False shame can cause more damage to your life than almost any other feeling.

Step Five: Enjoy how your body feels.
When it comes to feelings about your body, there is something else that can help you. God designed your body to experience pleasure in the world. God put more nerve endings in certain places like your

fingertips and feet. Their purpose is to quickly make you aware of where you are walking and what you are touching. You have physical feelings that God designed to encourage you to take care of your body.

We won't have time to fully go into the fact that God designed your body to feel pleasure during sexual intimacy. But Proverbs 5:18-19 describes what God has in mind for married couples: "May your fountain be blessed, and may you rejoice in the wife of your youth. A loving doe, a graceful deer—may her breasts satisfy you always, may you ever be captivated by her love." That's not the only place in the Bible that God tells us how great sex can be for married couples. He is the one who created our bodies to receive this kind of pleasure in sex. We hope you will trust that He designed you to wait until you are married to enjoy that kind of pleasure.

In fact, replacing meaning in life with a total focus on pleasure is why so many people get addicted to sex and drugs. People wouldn't use drugs if they produced only withdrawal, jail, and loss of money. They get started because they are pursuing pleasure. Drugs become an addiction because it takes more and more of the substance used more and more often to cover up the pain of withdrawal.

It's the same with sex. Sex addicts become that way because they are focused only on pleasure. God designed sex for pleasure, but also for so much more. The "more" is the meaningful relationship, bonding, and intimacy that God blesses you with in a healthy Christian marriage.

Your body was designed to give you pleasure in sensing God's beautiful world. As you take in the beauty of the world through your bodily senses, you might even be moved to praise God. Your body helps you sense and feel what is in the world around you.

I (Debi) will never forget the first time I praised God for His creation. Our youth group was driving from Florida to Jackson Hole, Wyoming. It was a grueling trip. I fell asleep somewhere along the way and woke up in the magnificent landscape of the Grand Tetons. As I opened my eyes to such majestic, mysterious mountain peaks, the first thought on my mind was, *How can anyone doubt that God made this?* The moon, the stars, the smell of a flower can make you think about how great God is.

God wants you to get pleasure from the food you eat. He didn't give us food just to meet our nutritional needs. In the Garden of Eden, God created the trees to be pleasing to the eye, too. You need to take time to touch, see, smell, and taste your food. Get comfortable knowing that you get a physical sensation when it's time to eat. It's okay to be hungry for a period. Even though I eat a good breakfast, sometimes I am mildly hungry by 10:30 A.M. In fact, if you do not feel hunger at all, you may be so out of touch with your body that you don't feel your physical feelings anymore. Anorexics ignore their hunger drive to the point that it subsides. This is just as damaging as never allowing your body to feel hungry by overeating or always eating at the first sign of hunger.

The sounds of nature can lift your spirit. I love the sound of waves crashing on the beach. Even the noise of insects can be musical. We get so busy that we often tune out these beautiful sounds that are all around us.

Learn to enjoy how your body feels. Think about the way you stretch when you first wake up. Remember how good it feels to release your muscles from their inactivity. Run your tongue across your just-brushed teeth and enjoy that feeling. Stop and smell the flowers rather than just walking by them. Identify the feeling of energy and strength by participating in healthy exercise.

As you enjoy how your body feels and how your senses help you take in the world around you, it will put you on better terms with your body. It makes you realize that there's more to think about in this world than worrying about being fat. You might even end up really believing that "you are fearfully and wonderfully made" (Psalm 139:14).

Step Six: Feel confident in your body.

There is absolutely no reason for you not to enjoy the body you have right now. So what if you are a little overweight? You can run, you can fly a kite, you can walk your dog. That's something to celebrate. You have a lot of reasons to feel confident about the body you have in the present.

In fact, when someone begins a change in diet or exercise by first accepting her body just the way it is, that person is more successful. Life can be good right now. Even if you have freckles or moles, even if your tummy isn't flat, even if you have ears that stick out, you are you and you are beautiful.

How did you feel as you read this chapter? Were you bored or intrigued? Did you feel stressed that you needed to get it done before your small group tonight? How do you feel now that you are almost finished? Do you agree that how you think produces what you feel? Try changing your thinking next time you are in a really bad mood and see if it works.

Rachel: A big breakthrough in my life has been to learn to live life in the moment. I used to just look forward to things I would do in the future like driving or college. This made me miss out on whatever stage I was in currently. You can have a great life right now—without being tan or losing 10 pounds.

Debi: One thing I like about being a woman is that I don't have to search hard for my feelings. But one thing that makes it hard to be a woman is that I am so quickly in tune with my feelings. I know the truth of how thinking right will help me with my feelings, but I still get angry, feel jealous, and get down sometimes. It's part of being human. I'm glad I understand how feelings work so I don't have to succumb to my moods. I can change the way I feel by changing the way I think.

Ideas to Help You Feel Good in Your Body

- Take a hot bubble bath and enjoy the sense of feeling your muscles relax and the feeling of being clean.
- Give yourself a manicure or pedicure.
- Go on a scent tour in a grocery store—smell flowers, produce, coffee, pastries. Enjoy the aromas all around you.
- Stand barefoot on a cold tile floor on a hot day, or warm yourself by a heater or fireplace in the winter.
- Feel textures in your room, from the desk you sit at to the soft pillow you lean on to the multi-angled pencil you write with.
- Perform different stretches while deep breathing and feel the release in your body.

WEEKLY CHALLENGE

Keep a diary of one way your body brings you pleasure each day. Try to think of a new one each day . . . a hug from your mom, running your fingers through your hair, bending over to touch your toes. It may seem cheesy, but it will help you learn to appreciate the wonderful body you have for reasons other than just how you look!

JUST BETWEEN GIRLS

1. What feeling does your body give you that you like best (examples: the sun on your skin at the beach, putting on lip gloss, getting a back rub)?
2. How can tuning into the pleasure senses that God created in your body help you praise Him?
3. How can overfocusing on pleasure lead to addiction? Has that ever happened to you?
4. Demonstrate (a cartwheel, handstand, touching your toes) or talk about some ways that you enjoy the feelings your body can take in.
5. What do you fear will happen if you let go of negative feelings about your body?
6. How would God comfort you in the fear you mentioned or comfort someone else about a fear they mentioned?
7. Give shoulder rubs around the room simultaneously. Tell the person doing yours how to make it feel better; for example, harder, softer, scratch lightly with fingernails.

CHAPTER FOUR

Girl World

 There has been a major revolution in girl talk in the past decade. Through my (Debi) teens and my first decade as a counselor I could totally relate to what women and teen girls were expressing when they described their bodies. But in the last 10 to 15 years the problem of body hate has taken a turn for the worse.

Our culture has given girls more to hate about their bodies than ever before. In the past, girls and women primarily obsessed about their weight, and if they focused on a specific body part, it was typically the breasts, nose, or hips. Not anymore. I asked Rachel to tell me some of the things girls talk about today concerning their bodies.

Rachel: We have names for our perceived body flaws now. My friends call the belly fat that hangs over low-rise jeans "pudge," but I've also heard it called "muffin top." Girls call thick ankles "crankles." "Chubb" describes kneecap fat. Girls worry about having a double chin, and one fate to be avoided is "mom arms." We criticize our bodies during our lunchtime conversations. It's as if each of us is trying to get the most pity for having the most pathetic body flaw. We constantly analyze what everyone is eating. Our daily conversations center on our food way too much.

Debi: It happens at every high school football game, every first day of school after a long summer, every gym period in the locker room. It's the girl greeting. When girls get together, they have to hug and talk about how cute everyone looks, or how tan they are, or how jealous they are about the outfits others are wearing. Women do it too. It's the way we bond. It seems to be a genetic predisposition in females, something like going to the bathroom in pairs. We dissect everything about the way we look in each other's presence.

Alison doesn't notice how much she talks about eating healthy food and working out. Her friends Mollie and Crystal want to get pizza after the game, but Alison says it's too late to eat junk like that. She reminds Mollie that she said she wanted to eat better. Crystal just rolls her eyes, which is Alison's invitation to begin explaining that the reason she is being the pizza Nazi is because there is so much wrong with her body. Alison points out the pudge hanging over her belt and her too-big thighs. Mollie and Crystal end up telling her how beautiful and perfect she is. The attempt to reinforce her beauty by reflecting on their respective body flaws begins and the conversation goes on from there.

It's just a normal girl conversation. Guys don't talk like that about their own bodies—and definitely not each others' bodies. Occasionally they might comment on big muscles, but that is about as far as it goes. Girls, on the other hand, are free to talk about the most intimate likes and dislikes about their bodies. It all feels so innocent, so natural to being a girl. But it does a lot to perpetuate the negative feelings we have about our bodies.

Another source that is ironically a little more damaging than peer-on-peer body bashing is moms bashing their own bodies. I'm (Debi) a mom and I want you to know that we do it without recognizing how we are hurting you. Often we don't even know that we are doing it. I was talking to the mother of a preschooler who realized she had to do something quick about her body image issues. It occurred to her after her five-year-old, who was trying on clothes in the dressing room, looked in the mirror and said, "I look fat in this." It's hard to admit as a mom, but she had to face the fact that her preschooler was hearing that statement from her own lips.

Moms hurt their daughters by bashing their own bodies. I agree with Naomi Wolf when she writes, "A mother who radiates self-love and self-acceptance actually vaccinates her daughter against low self-esteem."[1]

Moms also need to be respectful in talking about their daughters' bodies. We are so used to taking care of our daughters' bodies that we don't always realize the impact of our words. From the day you were born, it has been our job to feed you, to teach you how to care for your body, and to recognize when something's wrong with your body and get you help. Most of the time we don't mean to bash your body when we talk about your weight, your breakouts, or your clothing choices.

I try to encourage moms to make their homes a safe haven for their daughters so you don't have to hear what's wrong with your body when you are at home. You may have a mother who is totally unaware of how she is hurting you by the comments she makes about her body as well as yours. You should try talking to her about it and tell her how it makes you feel. If she doesn't change, you don't have to accept her comments in your soul. You can use the same tools we talked about with the names exercise to overcome the blows from her comments.

Qualities Girls Can Work on Developing

World Perspective—Learn about how other teens in the world live, especially in developing countries.

Friendliness—It's important to have your group of friends, but consider who you can include so you aren't too much of a clique.

Kindness—Practice acts of kindness. Let another driver go first, hold the door open for the person behind you, say "please" and "thank you."

Loyalty—Don't dump your old friends simply because you're included in a more popular crowd now.

Caring—Volunteer to help others through your church or another group.

Joy—You can have joy even when you aren't happy. It comes from trusting God even in hard times.

Contentment—Be creative with the makeup and clothes you have while coming up with new looks to put together.

Compassion—Care about others such as by helping with a special-needs child.

Intelligence—Don't play dumb so you won't threaten guys.

Respect of self and others—Respect teachers, even when you don't think they're great.

Forms of Body Bashing

Girl World involves many forms of body bashing. It can be as subtle as the way you talk about your own body or as dramatic as cutting.

Negative Body Talk

I want to challenge you to make a mental note of how often you say something negative about your own body in one week. You may not mean it when you say it; you probably say it to fit in with the other girls. Be particularly mindful when you are sitting down to eat with your friends. What do you talk about? How many calories there are in the candy bar you are scarfing down for lunch?

What would it be like for you to change the subject the next time the lunch table talk turns to calories or body bashing? Matthew 12:36 says, "But I tell you that men will have to give account on the day of judgment for every careless word they have spoken." Do you think body-bashing words would be considered "careless"?

Think about it. God made you. How does it feel to hear people tearing down with their cruel remarks something you made? God is big enough to still love you in spite of all your self-criticism. But when you are constantly putting your body down, it doesn't help you grow closer in your relationship with Him.

Sexual Sin

Paul makes an interesting point about sexual sin in 1 Corinthians 6:18: "Flee from sexual immorality. All other sins a man commits are outside his body, but he who sins sexually sins against his own body." It's a true statement. When you sin in your anger and yell at someone or steal from someone, you are not directly hurting your body in the way you are when you commit sexual sin. Paul is not saying that sexual sin is more unforgivable, just more irrational given that the results affect your own body.

Often a girl who has been a victim of sexual abuse will act out sexually. Part of the reason is that she felt so out of control when she was violated. She thinks she is in control because *she* is making the decision to act out sexually. Deep down she doesn't think she is worth anything, and that is why she exploits her own body. Sexual sin is a form of body bashing. It is not honoring the wonderful body God gave you.

I (Debi) think every teen should prayerfully consider what Paul writes in 1 Thessalonians 4:3-7 about avoiding sexual immorality:

> It is God's will that you should be sanctified: that you should avoid sexual immorality; that each of you should learn to control his own body in a way that is holy and honorable, not in passionate lust like the heathen, who do not know God; and that in this matter no one should wrong his brother or take advantage of him. The Lord will punish men for all such sins, as we have already told you and warned you. For God did not call us to be impure, but to live a holy life.

Paul was writing to people who became Christians after being part of a sexually promiscuous culture just like the one you live in. He gave instructions about how to think of yourself as a sexual being and how to decide what sexual behaviors you'll take part in before you are married. He says you should not give in to your own lusts, but even more than that, you are responsible for not causing your boyfriend (or other boys or men) to lust after you.

Perhaps you have made a commitment not to have sex before marriage, but you are becoming passionately involved with your boyfriend. I believe that teens who want to honor God's Word and truly want God's best for their lives should make a decision to only hug, kiss, or hold hands before marriage. This would be considered a weird decision in our culture, but it's a wonderful one to make.

Eating Disorders

Bulimia and anorexia were not words that I (Debi) knew the definition of when I was in high school. I never heard about them until college, and I didn't personally know anyone who had the disorders. I'm sure there were girls that were dealing with them, but no one talked about it. For me (Rachel), eating disorders are all around. It's even considered cool in some circles to be anorexic or bulimic. These issues are part of my daily life.

It's obvious that anorexics (girls who starve themselves and feel they can never be thin enough), bulimics (girls who binge and purge through throwing up and/or exercise), and bulimarexics (a combination of the two) hate their bodies.

For them, the rituals of not eating or bingeing and purging bring a sense of release from the pressure to be perfect (or other pressures). They do offer a payoff of some sort; otherwise girls wouldn't do it. But the payoff comes with a greater price to their health and well-being. I've (Debi) met many bulimics in my counseling experience who can't stop the binge-purge cycle even when it is causing them to *gain* weight, the opposite of why they started it in the beginning. Their behavior isn't keeping them thin, as they hoped it would, but they can't give it up.

The physical effects of anorexia and bulimia on the body can be life threatening. Heart damage can result in cardiac arrest. Bulimics are at risk of electrolyte imbalances. The stomach acid that washes over the teeth during frequent vomiting causes serious tooth decay. Other dangerous symptoms are malnutrition, dehydration, constipation, and abdominal pain.

Some girls are good at hiding eating disorders from others, but they can't hide them from their bodies. Their bodies will become the victims of body bashing and eventually be unable to sustain health. Unfortunately, some girls die from the damage these disorders cause to their bodies.

Obesity and Overweight

You hear enough about maintaining a healthy weight. We do not want to add to the voices that are constantly telling you to think about your weight, but obesity is a body bashing issue too. Often, girls who are overweight appear not to care about their bodies and what people think. That is not true. If you struggle with being overweight or obese, it may be due to genetic factors that perhaps make it easier for you to gain weight than the girl sitting next to you. But genetics are not the only factor. Just because your body was never designed to be a size eight doesn't mean that you should give up and not try to be the best weight for you.

When you give in to unhealthy eating and a sedentary lifestyle, you can expect to become overweight. If that's the case for you, you need to understand that your body is special and worth taking care of. You need to treat it well by eating well and taking part in physical activities that strengthen and tone your body, even if you will never be as thin as the world says you should be. Your goal should be a healthy size for you! Your doctor can help you determine if you are at a healthy weight for your height and age. If you are concerned about your weight, talk to your mom about the possibility of consulting a professional.

Cosmetic Surgery

Cosmetic surgery for teenage girls has been on the increase for several years. Girls who are not even fully developed are seeking breast augmentation to make themselves look "better." Liposuction and nose jobs are on the minds of many young girls. Reality television has reinforced the idea that every female should strive for perfection in all aspects of her body.

In a way, cosmetic surgery can become a type of body bashing. You are not accepting some things about yourself and you're bashing the way God made you. These comments by Debra Evans about cosmetic surgery are worth thinking about: "The type of 'healing' offered by some physicians today is a far cry from the wise norms that have guarded people's dignity and affirmed the value of human life in previous pagan cultures. . . . Might it partly be because beauty was never a medical problem to begin with, but because it's a holy riddle of God?"[2]

You can become so focused on what you hope to achieve from cosmetic surgery that you are not realistic about the risks. There is always a risk when you go under anesthesia, as people sometimes do not react well to it. You can also get infections, poor results, and lifelong complications from cosmetic surgery. People have even died from complications of elective surgeries.

This is not to say that no one should ever have plastic surgery. Sometimes people do have a legitimate need to correct physical problems. For example, plastic surgery is a wonderful gift when someone has suffered horrible burns or major trauma from an accident. Plastic surgeons have blessed people in developing countries by removing huge tumors and other medical abnormalities. However, this is not needless surgery for minor "imperfections." These are sometimes life-threatening conditions.

Drugs and Alcohol

Why do teenagers drink or try drugs? There are a variety of reasons. Not everyone who misuses alcohol or drugs will become addicted, but it is another example of body bashing. Most of the time a person chooses to drink or do drugs to fit in, escape, or find out where the fun is. Your body is God's temple, and any choice you make to mistreat it will be body bashing.

Cutting

Cutting, or the technical term *self-mutilating,* is yet another form of body bashing. This behavior has become more common with teenagers since it has been talked about more frequently on television and in magazines. Cutting used to be exhibited by individuals who were deeply depressed, had personality disorders, or were chemically depleted. Now it is associated with teens who are struggling with negative feelings, but who are not severely chemically depressed. It is yet another way that we humans try to handle our negative feelings.

I (Debi) have talked to people with deep psychological issues who deal with this addiction. I've also seen girls who had heard or read about it and tried it out in a desperate act to deal with their emotional pain. Sometimes I wondered if it was a cry for attention that would let others know that the individual was hurting. One author called it "the silent scream." If you cut yourself, I encourage you to find someone to talk to about it. Cutting never resolves the pain; its release is only temporary, then it's quickly replaced by shame. It is a vicious cycle.

Immodest Dressing

You may be surprised that we included this on our list of body bashing. It is so "normal" in our culture for girls to wear sexy, very revealing clothes. It's almost hard to find stylish clothes that aren't form fitting and immodest. Tight, clingy, low cut, and see-through clothes do not show respect for the body God gave you. When you dress like that, you are putting your body on display for people to evaluate or envy. Modesty became necessary after sin entered the world. Immodest dressing is a way of bashing your body by not respecting your sense of dignity. You can even become addicted to the attention dressing immodestly can give you.

On the popular television show *What Not to Wear*, women who dress immodestly are taught how to dress in a way that still shows off their femininity but isn't revealing. The experts on the show aren't coming from a Christian mindset as we are, but they want to show women how trashy they look (even from the world's standards) when they dress like that. Many times even after these women see how beautiful they can be in more modest attire, they go back to their old ways.

OTHER FORMS OF BODY BASHING

In a culture that worships bodies, we are seeing a rise in more forms of body bashing:

- Eating disorders in males, both anorexia and bulimia, are more frequently reported. As male bodies are idealized in the media, we will continue to see boys and men become more affected by the assault on their self-esteem as well.
- Steroids are a bigger temptation for males than females. Boys use them to enhance their athletic skills as well as their attractiveness. Steroids can be very dangerous.
- Body Dysmorphic Disorder, an irrational exaggeration of imagined body flaws, is a difficult psychological problem requiring treatment. This disorder is increasing as well.

HEALING YOUR SOUL . . . HEALING YOUR BODY

No matter what form of body bashing you may be involved in, true healing begins in your soul. Only then will you stop lashing out against your body in self-defeating ways. You heal your mind when you come to the place of understanding God's point of view about your body. You see His purpose, which is that your body will be a dwelling to house your soul.

A wrong body image is one way Satan got tripped up and took his horrible fall, which doomed him and caused us to live in a messed-up world. Ezekiel 28:12-14 describes how beautiful Satan was in all of creation.

You were the model of perfection, full of wisdom and perfect
in beauty. You were in Eden, the garden of God; every precious
stone adorned you: ruby, topaz and emerald, chrysolite, onyx
and jasper, sapphire, turquoise and beryl. Your settings and
mountings were made of gold; on the day you were created
they were prepared. You were anointed as a guardian cherub,
for so I ordained you. You were on the holy mount of God;
you walked among the fiery stones.

Satan was everything we humans want to be. He was the most
beautiful, he had a very special job, and he was blessed by God. Isaiah 14:11-15 describes Satan after his fall from grace:

> "All your pomp has been brought down to the grave, along with
> the noise of your harps; maggots are spread out beneath you and
> worms cover you. How you have fallen from heaven, O morn-
> ing star, son of the dawn! You have been cast down to the earth,
> you who once laid low the nations! You said in your heart, 'I will
> ascend to heaven; I will raise my throne above the stars of God;
> I will sit enthroned on the mount of assembly, on the utmost
> heights of the sacred mountain. I will ascend above the tops of
> the clouds; I will make myself like the Most High.' But you are
> brought down to the grave, to the depths of the pit."

Body worship led to Satan's downfall and it will destroy your soul as
well. God created Satan to be a beautiful reflection of His order and
nature. Satan got so caught up in how great he was that he tried to
be greater than God. He wasn't satisfied with the wonderful way God

had made him. If we are not careful, we will become dissatisfied. That is exactly what our society is telling us to do.

God has given us very specific information about how to live in our bodies while we are on earth. Our souls are healed through obeying God's Word regarding our bodies. Here are some of the things God tells you about your body that will help you keep it in perspective here on earth.

Don't worry about what your body needs; God will provide for you.

"Therefore I tell you, do not worry about your life, what you will eat or drink; or about your body, what you will wear. Is not life more important than food, and the body more important than clothes? Look at the birds of the air; they do not sow or reap or store away in barns, and yet your heavenly Father feeds them. Are you not much more valuable than they? Who of you by worrying can add a single hour to his life? And why do you worry about clothes? See how the lilies of the field grow. They do not labor or spin. Yet I tell you that not even Solomon in all his splendor was dressed like one of these. If that is how God clothes the grass of the field, which is here today and tomorrow is thrown into the fire, will he not much more clothe you, O you of little faith? So do not worry, saying, 'What shall we eat?' or 'What shall we drink?' or 'What shall we wear?' For the pagans run after all these things, and your heavenly Father knows that you need them." (Matthew 6:25-32)

How much time do you spend worrying about what you are going to wear, what you are going to eat, or what you are going to do? I

(Debi) want to challenge you to take God at His Word and stop worrying. Rather than worry, pray. That's what Philippians 4:6-7 teaches.

I can't tell you how many times God has provided just the clothes that I needed for a certain event. I'm not one to spend a lot of money on clothes—in fact, I love a good bargain! But there are certain places I go and events I attend for which I need the right clothes. Rather than worry or go into debt buying clothes that I can't afford, I pray about it. Many times God has picked out the perfect outfit at just the right price. While all the other ladies are wearing designer clothes, I'm decked out in clothes designed by God. (Okay, that's pretty cheesy, I'll admit.) But it will work for you. Learn to replace your worries about your body with prayer, and look for the ways God will answer.

As my (Rachel) senior prom approached, I didn't have a date or a dress. I had shopped way too long for the perfect dress. Finally, I started to pray about finding something. After another day of searching, I found a beautiful dress and a guy asked me to go with him. It was wonderful to look back and see how God provided for my needs. He even took care of the one I didn't specifically ask for—my date.

Don't worry about your body as much as about your soul.

> "Do not be afraid of those who kill the body but cannot kill the soul. Rather, be afraid of the One who can destroy both soul and body in hell. Are not two sparrows sold for a penny? Yet not one of them will fall to the ground apart from the will of your Father. And even the very hairs of your head are all numbered. So don't be afraid; you are worth more than many sparrows.

Whoever acknowledges me before men, I will also acknowledge
him before my Father in heaven." (Matthew 10:28-32)

Adolescence is a time of self-focus, but teens spend so much time
worrying about their bodies that they don't have time to focus on
their souls. The body you have is going downhill every minute of
every day! The evidence in my (Debi) body is more apparent than
yours, but it's true of you too. You will reach your peak fitness at age
18. There are things you can do to help yourself be physically fit at
every age. Think about the fact that you have only a short time on
this earth and that the body you are working so hard on now is not
going to last forever. We are all going to get new bodies, but your
soul is going to last forever. Your soul is what makes you you!

Our souls need a lot of attention. We can't see them in the mirror, but our souls are far from what they were created to be. Before
sin, Adam and Eve had the capacity to walk with God, to look into
His face, to fully take in His presence. After sin destroyed our relationship with God, the spiritual life became a journey toward tuning in to God's presence. The first step we take on this journey is
admitting that we are sinners and believing that Jesus is our salvation (see Romans 3:22-23 and John 3:16). After that we pray (both
asking things from God and listening to God), read the Bible as if
God is specifically telling us how to handle our problems, and practice spiritual disciplines such as worship, praying, and going on
retreats that will improve the condition of our souls and help us
draw closer to God.

It doesn't come naturally; you've got to work at listening to God
and taking in His presence. It's like trying to tune your radio when
you are on a country road. You know there's a station out there, but

you have to keep fine-tuning until you get it. I don't want you to think that it's work because God doesn't want us to find Him. That could not be further from the truth. It's work because our souls are so out of tune with God and so in tune with the world. Just being different from the world regarding body image will help you on your way.

Don't offer your body to sin; offer your body to God.

> In the same way, count yourselves dead to sin but alive to God in Christ Jesus. Therefore do not let sin reign in your mortal body so that you obey its evil desires. Do not offer the parts of your body to sin, as instruments of wickedness, but rather offer yourselves to God, as those who have been brought from death to life; and offer the parts of your body to him as instruments of righteousness. For sin shall not be your master, because you are not under law, but under grace. (Romans 6:11-14)

Did you know that you offer your body to sin when you ignore God's instructions for taking care of it? One of the most destructive ways teens sin against their bodies is acting out sexually. Another way you can offer your body to sin is by gossiping. You also sin with your body when you hold grudges deep inside. Teen girls sin by becoming so obsessed with how they look that they succumb to eating disorders, excessive spending, jealousy, and immodesty. You probably aren't consciously thinking, *I'm going to offer my body to sin today.* It is a result of subtle inner decisions that sometimes you are not even aware you are making.

The best way not to offer your body to sin is to consciously offer your body to God. You can say, "Okay God, here are my thighs. I offer them to You to run on the track team for Your glory." "God, I will take this broken-out face and go with my friend to visit her grandmother and cheer her up."

God has some great plans for you to serve Him while you live on earth with the exact body He gave you. Just do it!

God gives instructions about how we should treat our bodies and defines sexual sin.

> It is God's will that you should be sanctified: that you should avoid sexual immorality; that each of you should learn to control his own body in a way that is holy and honorable, not in passionate lust like the heathen, who do not know God.
> (1 Thessalonians 4:3-5)

As a teenager, the church taught me that God did not want me to have sex before marriage. but the church didn't do a good job of telling me what is okay sexually while dating. I was left without any instruction. When I asked God about this, He led me to 1 Thessalonians 4:3-8, which was mentioned earlier. I was in college and I decided to only hug, hold hands, and kiss a guy before marriage.

Scripture seemed to clearly say that any more involvement would make one or both of us want to have sex. I also knew I was sinning if I treated a guy in a way that made him want me like that. I encourage you to make decisions about what you believe God wants you to do and not do sexually while dating. Some girls decide not to even kiss. That's fine too. The main thing is that you not only need to determine what is too far for you, but also accept your responsibility not to wrong your brother by what you do!

Your body is temporary.

> Therefore we are always confident and know that as long as we are at home in the body we are away from the Lord. We live by faith, not by sight. We are confident, I say, and would prefer to be away from the body and at home with the Lord. So we make it our goal to please him, whether we are at home in the body or away from it. For we must all appear before the judgment seat of Christ, that each one may receive what is due him for the things done while in the body, whether good or bad. (2 Corinthians 5:6-10)

When Jesus returns to the earth or when you die, be ready to say good-bye to your body! Some people think of that with great relief. But you might be surprised how attached you have grown to your body. We think we will be able to recognize each other in some way. At that instant all of us will be free of all the body despair we ever had. Amen to that. In the meantime, it's good not to get so obsessed with your body on Earth. Begin to look at it as only temporary.

I (Rachel) have to remind myself of this from time to time, for example, when I have a special event coming and I have a pimple. It almost makes me feel like I want to stay home. That breakout may not go away in time for my event, but it is temporary and I learn how to live with it. There will come a time when we won't have breakouts at all. If we have a heavenly perspective, we can think of our bodies as temporary also. When we get to heaven, everything about them will be great.

You can glorify God with your body.

> I eagerly expect and hope that I will in no way be ashamed,
> but will have sufficient courage so that now as always Christ
> will be exalted in my body, whether by life or by death.
> (Philippians 1:20)

How do you glorify God with your body? I (Debi) glorify God as I use my mind and hands to write this book. I use my mouth to teach His Word at Bible studies. I reach out and give a welcoming hug to others. You can use your body to love and serve God too. It's as simple as giving up your seat to an elderly person or a pregnant woman. You can hold the door open for someone, especially mothers with strollers. When you do, you will be glorifying God with your body.

I (Rachel) use my body to glorify God when I play with a child, or sing with my voice, or use my ears to listen to my friends.

Your body will be transformed in heaven.

> Who, by the power that enables him to bring everything under
> his control, will transform our lowly bodies so that they will be
> like his glorious body. (Philippians 3:21)

We all want the perfect body. I've got good news for you. We are all going to get the perfect body someday. That day will come when our lowly bodies are transformed to be like His glorious body. Wow! That means we might move through walls like Jesus did in His resurrected body. We will eat and enjoy food as Jesus did. We might appear and disappear. I can't wait to find out. It's truly going to be great!

God instructs us to care for the bodily needs of people we can help.

> Suppose a brother or sister is without clothes and daily food. If one of you says to him, "Go, I wish you well; keep warm and well fed," but does nothing about his physical needs, what good is it? In the same way, faith by itself, if it is not accompanied by action, is dead. (James 2:15-17)

Have you noticed that there is always someone who has less than you? You may not like your out-of-date clothes, but there is someone in the world who would love to wear them. Are you aware of the physical needs that you can meet of people in this world? God expects you to be thinking of other people's bodily needs.

Several years ago I (Debi) gave up getting my nails done in order to support a child through Compassion International. Actually, it was a bargain because the monthly cost for Compassion was less than the monthly cost of nails. What I've gotten back are years of correspondence from a beautiful girl in the Philippines. And I have more time because I don't have my nails done twice a month.

Some girls grow out their hair and give it to Locks of Love.[3] Uncolored teen hair is ideal for this purpose. Ask God to show you a way you can help other people with their bodily needs, rather than be so focused on your needs. If you have extra money, why not support a child through a Christian feeding and education program. It's sad to think that the amount of money most Americans spend on their pets is more than whole families in developing countries make in a year. Could you give up one beauty regimen, such as acrylic nails or hair coloring, to help a child? It's something to think about.

The true healing our bodies need is forgiveness of sin, not a makeover.

> He himself bore our sins in his body on the tree, so that we might die to sins and live for righteousness; by his wounds you have been healed. (1 Peter 2:24)

More than anything else in this world, we need forgiveness of sin. Because of what Jesus did with His body, we can be forgiven. No matter how bad the sin is, God has an answer.

GOD HAS AN ANSWER

God can make anything in your life right. If you are willing to face the damage, God can heal whatever you may have done to your body. It could be negative body talk, a major eating disorder, or sexual promiscuity. Whatever it is, it's not too much for Jesus to heal. He heals you as you admit your sin and receive His righteousness.

Rachel: Our bodies truly are a gift from God. We all need to love our bodies because God created them. Part of loving our bodies is respecting them with our choices.

Debi: You live in Girl World every day. It is the culture of what it means to be a girl. Girls will always be concerned about their looks and that is okay, but don't let it get out of hand. Recognize body bashing for what it is and put your body in perspective. It will bring you great freedom in life.

WEEKLY CHALLENGE

Ask God to help you remember all the ways that you have not trusted Him and have bashed your body. Write them down. Ask God to forgive you and help you stop bashing your body. Tear up the list, or burn it as a way of visualizing that God totally forgives you and gives you a new start.

JUST BETWEEN GIRLS

1. In what ways do you see girls bashing their bodies?
2. How have you been a body basher?
3. What does it mean to offer your body as an instrument of sin? (Romans 6:11-14)
4. What do you think a glorious body is going to be like?
5. What should we worry about concerning our souls? (Matthew 10:28-32)
6. Who has some bodily or physical needs you can meet?
7. Have one girl stand up in front of the group. Go around the group having each person say the girl's name and repeating what God says about her from this list until every statement is made. For small groups, each girl will make two or three statements. Repeat the exercise for every girl present.

_____, your body is a temple of God.

_____, you were wonderfully made.

_____, you were knit together by God Himself.

_____, nothing about your body is unknown to God.

_____, God saw your body before you were even born.

_____, God knows the number of days you will live in your body.

_____, you are created in the image of God.

_____, God knows the very number of hairs on your head.

_____, your true beauty comes from your inner self.

_____, you can exalt Christ in your body.

_____, God knows everything your body needs.

_____, because of what Christ did with His body, you are without fault.

_____, you are forgiven.

_____, you are accepted.

_____, there is no condemnation toward you.

_____, you are beautiful!

(Genesis 1:27; Psalm 139:13-16; Matthew 6:25-33; Luke 12:7; Romans 8:1; 2 Corinthians 6:16; Philippians 1:20; 1 John 1:9)

CHAPTER FIVE

Not Just a No Body

It is our pleasure to inform you that you are the winner of a full body makeover. Your application has been accepted for participation in a new study on teens and cosmetic surgery. Some of the world's top physicians, trainers, dentists, designers, and dermatologists, all willing to fulfill any dream you have for your body, are completely at your disposal. There is no limit to the cost or what you can have done.

Since this is make-believe, let's also imagine there is no pain involved either. You can have operation after operation and nothing will ever hurt. Every decision you make will be carried out to your exact specifications without side effects or the possibility of something going wrong. Do you choose to accept your prize?

Did you choose to turn down the prize because you accept the body God designed for you? The preceding two paragraphs were a test. Did you find yourself salivating for such an opportunity? I (Debi) hope not. I'm hoping instead that you recognize the trap that becoming overly obsessed with your body can be. I'm hoping that reading the Scriptures, talking with friends, and beginning to like your body is helping you know the freedom of being yourself. It would be so wonderful to know that you would turn down the opportunity to totally transform your body if it were offered to you.

I (Rachel) told my mom that a lot of us would still have chosen the body makeover. But since we know it's just a dream, let's look at reality.

There is a delicate balance of living here on earth in a body. God created our bodies in such a way that they require time and attention. If we can't take care of them properly, our teeth will fall out, our gums will get infected, our hair will become a tangled, greasy mess—and oh, the smell. Here's a way to consider the need for body care. Go on a 30-hour bus ride. Take a picture of yourself before you leave and one after you arrive. Are you getting (and smelling) the picture?

As King David writes, "We are dust" (Psalm 103:14). Our bodies are dying and will be destroyed at some point. God plans to give us new bodies in heaven.

The body you've got is the only one you will get here on earth, and it has to last you for as long as you live here. It's important to take care of it. Do you really respect your body? What if Jesus were to stand before you and say, "I gave you this body for your time on earth. I picked out the color of your eyes and the exact way you were made." He might ask you, "Do you like your body and understand how it will help you love and serve Me?" Another question He might have for you is, "How are you caring for your body?" What would you say?

Brianna imagined being asked this question by Jesus, and she was a little sad to face the facts. The reality was that she did not like her body at all. She avoided mirrors as much as she could. She didn't wear makeup or do much to her hair, all in an effort to avoid seeing herself. She was a big girl at 5'11" and a good weight for her would have been 160 pounds. She hated how much more she weighed than her friends, yet she didn't want to starve herself, so she just stopped caring. She paid little attention to eating well and living an active life. Before long, she ballooned up to over 200 pounds. She told herself that she was fat and happy, not always trying to starve herself like stupid girls did. In reality, shame and disgust followed her everywhere. She hated herself so much she couldn't imagine how God could love her.

It's not good to starve yourself, but it's not good to stop caring about your body either. God gave you a body that does require a certain amount of care and maintenance.

God Formed You with His Hands

I (Debi) love the account of the creation of the world. I acknowledge that it is still a mystery, but I believe that this earth and the universe surrounding us are a creation of a holy God! Every new scientific discovery convinces me more and more that this is a world ordered by a Being more amazing than I can fully imagine.

There's something about the creation story (Genesis 1) I never noticed until a Bible teacher pointed it out to me. When God began the creation of our universe, He spoke it into being. God said, "Let there be light." And there was light. Day after day, for six days, He followed the same pattern. He said, "Let there be land." "Let the land produce vegetation." "Let there be stars, moon, and sun in the sky." "Let there be living creatures in the waters." "Let the land produce animals." God said it, and created it; everything came into existence by the power of His words.

What a miracle! Do you believe that our wonderful God created the universe with the power of His Word?

Well, it gets more amazing than that. God did not merely speak mankind into being as He had done with the vegetation and the animals. When He decided to make man, He formed man with His very hands and breathed into man the breath of life. He made man in His own image (Genesis 1:26). This amazing Creator God actually used His hands to reach down into the dust and form a man (Genesis 2:7). You are His workmanship; your very body was created by Him (Ephesians 2:10). After God formed the man from the dust, He went even further and breathed into man the breath of life, which contains the very image of God (Genesis 2:7).

It is very important that you understand that your body was formed by God. You will gain a broader appreciation for your body and your God when you fully grasp that He made you! Job understood this about himself. He said, "Your hands shaped me and made me" (Job 10:8).

Accepting that you were formed by God is the beginning of deep faith. Look at your hands and think about this: God formed those hands; He is proud of those hands. Each day, look at your hands and say, "God is proud of what He made."

God not only made you, He made you for a purpose. Isaiah 43:21 says, "The people I formed for myself that they may proclaim my praise." God formed you so you could praise Him. David did this in Psalm 139:14 when he said, "I praise you because I am fearfully and wonderfully made." Do you praise God for how He made you?

Another verse that explains why we have the thighs we have, or the nose, or the height is Ephesians 2:10: "We are God's workmanship, created in Christ Jesus to do good works, which God prepared in advance for us to do." He gave you those muscular thighs so you can stand strong when you are working with your friends on the Habitat for Humanity house.

In Isaiah 49:5 the prophet says that he was formed by God: "He who formed me in the womb." Don't think you cannot possibly have been formed by God because you are generations away from Adam. God was intimately involved in forming Adam, and He also formed you just the way He wanted to make you.

The goal of our spiritual journey is to get in touch with how safe and trusting God's hands are and to rest in them as Jesus did. From the cross He spoke, "Into your hands I commit my spirit" (Luke 23:46, Psalm 31:5). It takes true faith to believe that you were formed by God for a purpose. It is the beginning of deeper faith. Jesus can teach us about how to take care of our bodies without becoming obsessed with them because He lived in a body too.

JESUS LIVED IN A BODY

Jesus lived in a body when He came to the earth. For 33 years He humbled Himself by taking on human flesh. He knew that He would die prematurely, but that didn't stop Him from taking the best care He could of His body. Actually, it was good that He took care of His body while He lived on earth. If He hadn't, He would not have been strong enough to die for us on the cross.

Remember that beating He was given before He was crucified? That lashing killed a lot of men. Jesus was able to live through that, walk to Golgotha carrying a heavy cross part of the way, and hang on the cross for six hours before dying. He had to be in top physical condition to have completed His mission, which resulted in our great salvation.

You could say that Jesus ate health food. Whenever He fed others in the gospels, He always gave fish and whole grain bread. He ate a Mediterranean diet Himself, which was rich in fiber and protein. If you measure the distance between the towns that Jesus walked to, you will realize that he was aerobically fit. He also had been a carpenter for most of His life, which required Him to be strong. He didn't lift weights, but His daily labor involved what would be equal to strength-training workouts.

It really does matter to God that we take care of our bodies. He doesn't want us to be obsessed with them, but He does want us to care for them. He gave human beings bodies that needed a certain degree of care even before sin entered the world. We know from Genesis 1–2 that Adam and Eve ate food daily while they lived without sin in the garden.

TAKING CARE OF YOUR BODY

The only one who can truly take care of your body is you. Your parents can help you or sabotage your efforts. Your friends can encourage you, but it all comes down to you. When I (Debi) talk to parents of preschool and school-age children, I encourage them to teach their children how to eat correctly at the dinner table. Children rely on adults to make food choices for them. The best way to learn to eat properly is by observing what is served to you at your own kitchen table.

Your parents may or may not have taught you to eat in a healthy manner. Many kids are growing up without these wonderful family experiences. If your parents cook at home and ask you to sit at the table and eat with your family, you have been blessed.

If you don't have that good fortune, let us fill you in on the basics. But we don't do this to make you obsess over how to eat. Researchers at the University of Minnesota found that boys and girls who frequently read articles about dieting and weight loss were more likely to follow extreme eating behaviors than those who knew little about food and calories.[1] Most individuals with eating disorders I counseled knew almost as much about food as a licensed nutritionist. We don't want you to turn into a food expert. We simply want to give you some common sense tips to follow—but not ritualistically.

Common Sense Eating

Every day you should eat from the five food groups—grains, fruits and vegetables, protein, fats, and dairy. You need a lot of grain; whole-grain cereal in the morning and for snacks is a great way to get started on grains. Choose whole-grain bread too.

Eat 5 to 9 servings of fruits and vegetables each day. A fruit for breakfast and a fruit and vegetable for both lunch and dinner are great ways to get at least five in. Follow the 3/4 plate rule. When fruits and vegetables cover 3/4 of your plate, you are keeping your food groups in balance.

Eat protein twice a day. Get your protein mainly from meat products. Try to choose white meats and lower fat meats when you can.

Make sure you get dairy through milk, cheese, and yogurt. During your teen years you form the bone matrix you will need as you age, and you build it by the calcium you take in. Calcium comes mainly from dairy products.

You might be surprised to learn that you need some fat in your diet. Choose good fats such as avocados, nuts, and olive oil, and don't overdo it.

Some people eat better when they eat smaller portions every three hours. This isn't always possible while at school, though.

Let's talk about other ways you can focus on your body without getting out of balance. In 1 Peter 3:3-4 Peter writes to women, "Your beauty should not come from outward adornment, such as braided hair and the wearing of gold jewelry and fine clothes. Instead, it should be that of your inner self, the unfading beauty of a gentle and quiet spirit, which is of great worth in God's sight."

God knows that we women like to wear beautiful things and make ourselves look good. In the Bible, you never find instructions to men about wearing gold jewelry, fine clothes, and fixing their hair. God tells us to keep our body care in balance with our love for Him. Even the choices we make in hair, makeup, and clothes send a message to others that we love God.

First Timothy 2:9-10 says, "I also want women to dress modestly, with decency and propriety, not with braided hair or gold or pearls or expensive clothes, but with good deeds, appropriate for women who profess to worship God." Do you dress modestly? Do you dress decently? Could people who don't know you, who are just looking at you from across the room, think that you are a girl of propriety by the way you dress?

Do you know what the word *propriety* means? It means polite, correct, appearing as expected of her. When you get dressed in the morning, ask yourself, "Does this clothing choice communicate that I am a decent and proper girl?"

Again, beauty isn't just what you do on the outside. That's important to remember, and we will address how to keep beauty in balance. Before you ever put on clothes or wash your face, the most important beauty treatment you can have is a smile that springs up from deep in your soul. This is the kind of inner, unfading beauty that is of great worth in God's sight.

One of the best ways to become beautiful is to fully accept yourself and believe that you have value and worth. We are praying that every girl who reads this book will experience this beauty treatment.

Accepting herself was a huge step for Brianna. She had to stop thinking that she was too big to be a girl. She began to think, *I'm a big, beautiful girl and I have value and worth right now at 200 pounds.* She made an inner change that began to show on the outside. She decided to join a Weight Watchers group to learn how to eat in balance again and to have accountability. After she lost 40 pounds (it took six months), she was tempted to try to cut back more to lose extra weight, but she realized that was a trap too. She kept working on being happy with how God made her.

Hair

How much money do you spend on your haircuts and hair products? Hair is an important part of a woman's appearance. If you cut your hair short, it means frequent trips to the hairstylist. Girls love to experiment with hair color, but keep in mind that you have a hair color that was picked out for you personally. Is it worth the money and maintenance to change your hair color, or would there be more freedom if you just wore your natural color?

I (Debi) color my hair every 12 to 14 weeks. I do it because I am graying, but not gray enough to let gray be my natural color. Just think, you are going to be my age sooner than you think, and you will probably want to color your hair then. This is a time you can enjoy not having to go to the bother of coloring your hair. Why not fully enjoy it?

If you do color your hair, think ahead to maintenance. My (Rachel) friend is really smart about the way she colors her hair. She decided to highlight it so it's a brighter blonde rather than coloring overall. With highlights it doesn't look totally awful at the roots if she can't get in to have it done or if she is a little low on money. She also saves money by choosing a shade that is really close to her natural color because that also helps her reduce her trips to the salon.

Do you keep your hair clean and styled? Do you give it the attention it needs? At your age, you probably need to wash your hair more frequently than adults or children because of the excess oil in your skin and scalp. Find a great shampoo and conditioner that keep your hair looking clean and healthy.

One possible way to interpret the scripture about braiding hair

(1 Timothy 2:9) is to not do things with your hair that take hours and hours to create and maintain. Find a way to style your hair that doesn't cut into your ability to spend time with God. Many teens need to wash and dry their hair every day. What shortcuts can you take so that you can spend time with God in the morning and still have clean hair?

A good idea for teens is to have a hairstyle that will still look good if you have a late night, oversleep, or just don't want the trouble of styling it every day. A ponytail is an example.

Skin

You must develop good hygiene habits because you have more oil on your skin in the teen years than at any other time in your life. Pores can get clogged. Explore a skin-care regimen that works for you without costing too much money.

Consider the cost of beauty treatments in light of the problem you have. It's really sad that most girls these days would spend thousands of dollars on doctors and products designed to get rid of normal breakouts. Some teens have a legitimate acne problem and do need expensive treatments. But most kids have normal blemishes that can be treated with proper hygiene and good over-the-counter products.

Those who are unwilling to have the smallest breakout opt for expensive and invasive options. Some of these treatments can have long-term effects. For example, overuse of antibiotics to treat minor skin problems can make them ineffective when you have a serious or life-threatening infection. Think about how you want to take care of your skin. What is the most cost-efficient way?

Be careful when applying moisturizer. While skin care programs recommend it, teens have so much oil naturally that moisturizers can make it worse. Look for the term *noncomedogenic* on your moisturizer; this indicates that it won't clog your pores. Be faithful to wash and cleanse your face two times a day. One of the best things you can do for your skin is to drink plenty of water.

Following are acne skin-care guidelines from the American Academy of Dermatology. If you follow these and still have a problem you can't resolve, seek the help of a dermatologist, family physician, or other professional.

Acne Skin-care Guidelines

- Don't squeeze acne because it spreads inflammation.
- Wash your face twice a day with a mild cleanser and pat dry. Don't scrub vigorously.
- Look for cosmetics and toiletries labeled "noncomedogenic" (does not clog pores).
- Keep oily hair away from acne areas by tying it back while sleeping, and don't use oils on your scalp.
- Avoid exposure to sunlight and tanning beds.
- Don't expect instant results. Give the product enough time to work.[2]

Diet

You should be aware of your diet, but we teens need to be careful about overdoing it. I (Rachel) am almost scared to worry about what I eat sometimes because I wonder if I am starting some bad habits that could lead to anorexia or bulimia. I do need to put some thought into eating right. The media are constantly enticing us with fattening and unhealthy foods, and because teens have a higher metabolism, we can eat more junk food without gaining weight. However, there is an important balance we need to maintain in our food-obsessed/thin-obsessed society.

The teen years are about hanging out with friends and having fun enjoying foods such as popcorn and pizza. When teens get together, junk food is usually on the menu. That's good in a way. You need to let yourself have fun and bond with your friends over ice cream. It doesn't hurt to opt for a salad every now and then either.

If you are like Brianna and trying to better care for your body, it's sometimes hard to spend time with friends. Don't make a big deal about what they are eating and what you are eating. You can choose a salad even at a fast-food restaurant. Do the best you can without overfocusing on food.

If you are tying to cut out a few calories, try to stop drinking soft drinks. When I (Rachel) got into high school, I began having a Coke at lunch, one for a snack, and whenever I went out to eat. I realized that I started gaining weight after only a few months. I had a friend who stopped drinking soft drinks and lost 20 pounds. I decided to drink more water and tea, and I felt a lot better. I still have soft drinks occasionally, but I usually get a diet, and save the 10 teaspoons of sugar for another type of food.

Clothes

God wants us to enjoy fashionable clothes without obsessing over them. It's not a sin to know the latest fashion. It is a sin to think about clothes too much, though. I (Rachel) do look at trends and try to choose the ones that I think will look good on me. I don't buy something just because it is new this season if it doesn't flatter my body type. When I do buy a trendy item, I try not to spend a lot of money on it. There are always knock-off versions available that can be fun and inexpensive.

Another way to save money on clothes is to buy the tops or

Tips on Dressing Modestly

- Bend over in front of the mirror to check if your cleavage shows. If it does, your shirt is too low cut.
- Check in a full-length mirror to make sure your shorts cover your whole bottom.
- Wear a long tank top under a shorter top without showing skin.
- Make sure your skirts or dresses are at least as long as or longer than your fingertips when your hands are down by your sides.
- Check out how high slits on dresses and skirts go up—especially when you're sitting.
- Is it see-through? Wear something under it.
- Is it clingy? Wear a jacket over it.
- If you have a healthy relationship with the males in your family, ask your dad or brother if he thinks what you are wearing is okay.
- Modesty isn't just about clothes; it includes makeup, actions, and hair too.

shirts that you wear under jackets at a discount store rather than the mall. You don't have to buy the whole outfit at the same place. Think about whether you already have a white shirt at home that will go under that sweater, or whether you can get it for a better price at a different store.

Modesty is a huge issue regarding clothes these days. The clothes that are designed for teens are very revealing and exploit girls' bodies. You have to be a good shopper to find stylish clothes that are modest. Don't give up. Set your standards high and keep shopping until you find clothes that will work. Sometimes you have to think outside the box. In fact, I (Rachel) have to shop in the boys department to get shorts that are required for the mission trips at my church. I cannot find mid-thigh-length shorts in the junior girls department.

WHAT ABOUT BODY PIERCING AND TATTOOS?

I (Debi) hate this question, but I know it is important to bring up because piercing and tattoos are so common in our society today. I, like most parents, would never want my child to have body piercings or tattoos, although Rachel does have her ears pierced. My best advice is to decide now to wait until you are 25 to get a tattoo or do body piercing. By that time, you will know if it is something you really want to do and not just something you did because everyone else was doing it.

Try to project such a permanent effect into the future. What will it be like to have a hole through your belly button when you are nine months pregnant? What will that tattoo communicate to a future boss someday? How will that tattoo down your arm look with a lacy wedding gown? How will it look on a 60-year-old woman?

Have you considered the possibility that you could contract a disease such as hepatitis C if tattoo equipment is not properly sterilized? Should you decide in the future that you don't like your tattoo anymore, its removal is expensive and not guaranteed. Think about those things before you do something so permanent to your body.

TALKING TO GOD

Again, God knows that you need clothes to wear. He is not opposed to your looking good and having the right clothes to fit the occasion. He knows that you need a prom dress.

Have faith. Ask Him to help you find the clothes that you need. Ask Him to lead you to the best buys, or pray specifically for a certain outfit that you need. Talk to Him while you are getting dressed. Ask for His help in deciding what you are going to wear each day. God wants to be involved in every aspect of your life. Getting dressed is something you do every day. Use that as time to fellowship with God and ask Him to help you dress in a way that pleases Him.

The aftereffects of Hurricane Katrina (2005) in the city of New Orleans taught me (Debi) a great deal about how fragile our bodies really are. I don't often think about the fact that I am so dependent on a simple thing like water to stay alive. God has provided for my earthly body so adequately that I take my daily provisions for granted. As I thought of those people dying in the Superdome, I realized that had I been trapped there, I could have died too.

It was a lesson in humility and gratefulness. My daily needs are part of the prayer Jesus taught us to pray: "Give us this day our daily bread." There is a faith connection between my daily needs and God. I think one reason He gave us bodies that are not completely self-sufficient is so we will rely on Him and have the opportunity to grow in faith each day.

Rachel: Modesty is such an issue for teenagers in our world today. I challenge you to take what you've learned from this chapter and apply it to your life. I know it's hard in our culture, but I have no doubt God will bless you for your obedience.

Debi: Nobody can avoid addressing body issues. We can spend our lives being ashamed of the body we have and mistreating it, or we can responsibly accept and care for our body as part of our spiritual journey. I hope you are learning that your body is special and that you can connect to God by bringing your daily needs to Him.

WEEKLY CHALLENGE

Each morning pray about what you will wear and how you will do your hair. Talk to God about how you are taking care of your body. Ask Him for strength to eat right and be disciplined to exercise as you planned.

JUST BETWEEN GIRLS

1. What does it mean to you that God formed you with His hands?
2. Share a body-care secret that works for you. What's a product or item or routine that helps you care for your body?

3. What do you think Jesus enjoyed most about having a body?

4. What do you think Jesus enjoyed least about having a body?

5. What do you enjoy most about having a body?

6. What do you enjoy least about having a body?

7. What similarities between our earthly bodies and heavenly bodies do you think there will be?

CHAPTER SIX

Start a New Beauty Trend

 As you can see from the secular books, magazines, and Web sites we've quoted, even the world sees the problem with the epidemic of girls who are concerned only about getting attention for their bodies.

The world will eventually grow weary of the pursuit of perfect bodies and empty lives. Perhaps a trend of modesty and uniqueness is bubbling up from the insane place that body worship has led us. We are hoping you will join us in starting a trend toward wholeness. It's always helpful to know there are others out there who accept your same values. Let's bring a little sanity to the small place on the planet we each inhabit. Perhaps we will begin a trend that will last.

TRENDS BEGIN WITH BREAKTHROUGHS

Words can be deadly to the soul. Words also have the power to heal. We've written this book to give you opportunities to hear and speak healing words. Mainly we have spoken God's words to you. What God has to say about our bodies is contrary to what the world says. We hope you and your group are beginning to use God's Word to affirm yourself and each other.

Has this study helped you understand that we girls all want the same thing? Do you now recognize some of the crazy ways we try to get love? Do you see that much of our body worship is an attempt to get people to affirm us? Do you understand that the only way back to wholeness is to believe that God has all the affirmation we will ever need?

God's Word is full of healing power. Hebrews 4:12 says, "For the word of God is living and active. Sharper than any double-edged sword, it penetrates even to dividing soul and spirit, joints and marrow; it judges the thoughts and attitudes of the heart."

His Word can set us free from the traps of body hate. We all want to be affirmed and liked just the way we are. We need to know that we are totally valuable and we are God's precious, beautiful daughters. Whether we have flat chests, thick thighs, or frizzy hair, we are all loved, wanted, and chosen by God. He has a lot to say about our bodies.

GOD'S WORD AND OUR BODIES

God knows humans are tempted to overemphasize how a person looks in evaluating his or her character. It's nothing new to God that people will overemphasize outward appearance. In fact, when Israel was looking for a king to replace King Saul, God knew that Samuel would never believe that David was the one He wanted him to anoint as king. God warned Samuel ahead of time that he shouldn't look just on the outside, but should look on the heart as God does (1 Samuel 16:7).

God is not into beauty the way we are. If He were, He would have made each of us look like Barbie and Ken dolls. He thinks we are beautiful just the way we are. You may go through this life not measuring up to the standard of beauty held by your peers, but that doesn't mean God didn't make you beautiful.

David was described as "ruddy." That means he was red from the sun and heat from being outside with the sheep. When Samuel called him up from the fields, he didn't think this ruddy boy would be the king of Israel. But Samuel knew the difference between his thoughts and God's thoughts, and there was no denying it: God was telling him to anoint David as King.

God knows that other people judge and evaluate you by your looks. Keep in mind that God does not use the same guidelines as *People* magazine to consider whether you are beautiful or not. Don't

---

What God Values in a Girl
love, joy, peace
kindness, patience, self-control
gentleness, faithfulness, goodness

What Magazines Value in a Girl
thinness, clothes, no blemishes
white teeth, sex appeal, great hair
diet, makeup, jewelry, handbags

waste your life trying to live up to the evaluation of man. For some of you, your relationship with God may be the only place your body is affirmed.

Some of you live in homes that are as negative about your body as the advertising industry. We encourage you to reread this book and reach out to your church family to receive the help you need to accept God's truth! Having said that, even if your church rejects your body, pray that God will bring you someone who can help you believe that what He says about you is true. (Unfortunately this body hate has infiltrated the good sense of church leaders as well.)

If you could choose how your body was going to look, wouldn't you try to make yourself the most attractive person around? Obviously, physical attraction is not all that important to God. Jesus could have looked any way that God desired for Him to look. God chose not to give Jesus qualities and an appearance that would attract people to Him. Still, people loved Him and followed Him. They found Him beautiful as they got to know Him because He was so beautiful in spirit. It's just not important to God that you are the most attractive person in the world. It is important to Him that you are attractive in your spirit.

There is more to life than being attractive! It's huge in our culture, but trying to be beautiful can distract you from what your life is really all about. God took extra care to make Jesus look the way He did, and He has done the same for you! You are uniquely designed by the one true Creator. You are His masterpiece.

God knows we females are particularly interested in making ourselves look nice (1 Peter 3:3-4). God never puts us down for caring about being outwardly beautiful. He just tells us to keep it in balance. It is not as if you cannot look your best and be a Christian. God doesn't want you to let your adorning merely be on the outside. He wants you to look on the inside of you. He wants you to put on a beautiful spirit.

Do you know what a beautiful spirit looks like? Mother Teresa and Princess Diana died within weeks of each other. Both were known worldwide to be beautiful women of compassion and care for the needy. They had even joined efforts in helping others. Princess Diana fit the world's standards of beauty and style. She was one of the most photographed women of the world. Why did the cameras follow Mother Teresa, you may wonder. She radiated the beauty of one who is totally in love with God. She couldn't help but charm the world by her spiritual attractiveness.

A beautiful spirit is being self-confident without pride. It is being well-groomed without being obsessed with your looks. It is being content without being greedy. It's fine to wear nice clothes and be well-groomed as long as you keep this in balance with other qualities (Proverbs 31:22).

The Proverbs 31 woman was clothed in fine purple, the designer clothes of her day. You'll notice that her clothing was mentioned in the context of all her other wonderful qualities. Her clothing was the only thing mentioned about her outward appearance. In other words, it's great to look nice and wear the best clothes you can within your budget, but your appearance needs to be kept in balance with everything else in your life. You can be a well-dressed person without being obsessed with your looks.

What we think we look like on the outside depends on how we feel about ourselves in general. In Song of Songs 1:6, the bride of

Solomon is complaining about her body "flaw." She hates how dark her skin has gotten because she had worked in the vineyards.

Solomon could have chosen as his bride a woman who hadn't turned brown from the sun. Obviously, he never noticed this "flaw" that she felt was so awful. It's interesting to note in 2:1 that she has stopped obsessing about her body flaw. She calls herself the Rose of Sharon. She is able to accept her true beauty.

That's the goal of this study. Some of your body flaws are really just part of your unique design. When you know you are loved, you'll feel less need to make your hair curly, or your teeth perfectly white, or get rid of your round bottom. Though none of that changes, you'll feel beautiful!

Have you ever considered that you can be outwardly beautiful and still be unattractive to others? Proverbs 11:22 says, "Like a gold ring in a pig's snout is a beautiful woman who shows no discretion." A beautiful person with a bad disposition pales in comparison with a regular looking person who has good character.

Don't we all know someone who fits this description? She may possess attractive outward qualities, but we are repelled by her character. Beauty and charm are not nearly as appealing as a woman who knows who she is to God and lives for Him. Loving God will bring out your deepest beauty. Proverbs 31:30 says, "Charm is deceptive, and beauty is fleeting; but a woman who fears the LORD is to be praised."

A WORD ABOUT DISCRETION

A few years ago an 18-year-old girl from our former hometown went to Hollywood. She was following her dream of being a star and was cast as a girlfriend on a major sitcom. If things went well, she would become a regular. It is very rare to have this kind of dream come true after such a relatively short time. After she taped the first two shows, the media used the fact that she had posed for *Playboy* to fill the entertainment gossip columns. She was written off the show. That was literally the end of her career. Even in our immoral culture, it is still taboo for a serious actress to pose for *Playboy* and have a chance to "make it" in Hollywood.

If the world thinks a woman without discretion loses, shouldn't a Christian have even higher standards? God decided that our bodies are the best temple for Him to dwell in (1 Corinthians 6:19). One reason to take care of your body is that, if you are a Christian, the Holy Spirit lives in your body with you. The prophets who wrote that the Holy Spirit would actually come to live in believers couldn't really grasp what we now know firsthand. All who are believers in Jesus Christ actually have God's presence in our very souls. This is such a great honor.

It is so fascinating to think that God actually dwells in our hearts after we consider how He came to dwell in the temple on earth. In the Old Testament, King Solomon built a permanent temple to house the Ark of the Covenant in the city of Jerusalem. His father, King David, had made it his lifelong dream to build this temple. He had collected the most exquisite building supplies to get the process started, and Solomon added to what his father had done. The most talented artisans had contributed to this decade-long project.

When the temple was all finished, it was time to bring the Ark of the Covenant into the temple and invite the presence of the Lord to dwell there. Second Chronicles 7 records the events of that special day. Solomon prayed that God would fill the temple. And God's answer was that He would. God's glory filled the temple and immediately there was a revival. Sacrifices were offered to God's glory as never before. Solomon and David and all the individuals involved spent so much of their money, time and dreams on that temple, but it would not have been complete if God had not chosen to dwell there.

Now God has chosen to dwell in you. Everywhere you go, every party you attend, you are taking the Holy Spirit with you. You are the temple of God.

Our body hate is such an insult to God. We truly insult Him when we reject what He made. We're not trying to make you feel overly guilty for not liking your body. God loves us in spite of our insults. In fact, at the exact moment the Roman soldiers were nailing Him to the cross, Jesus asked God to forgive them. We hope that you will discover that really learning to love and respect your body is a way that you praise and honor God.

I (Debi) have thought about these concepts through the years. I believe that liking your body and understanding that you were formed by the very hand of God are foundational to your faith. I grew up in a world less obsessed with beauty than the world you're living in today. Most teens reading this book have never known a time when grandmas looked like grandmas and mothers looked like mothers and daughters looked like daughters. I did live in that kind of world, and it was a sweeter place.

It's important that we believe that God made us, saved us, and has a purpose for our lives on earth before we live with Him for eternity in heaven. Accepting how you look is coming in balance with

God and showing that you believe He knows what He is doing even when you can't see it. These words from David Foster are a reminder of what a marvelous creation our bodies are:

> You are a living example of God's commitment to excellence. In His superlative and exquisite design, He gave you a multi-billion-dollar body governed by several hundred systems of control, each interacting with and affecting the other. For example, your brain has 10 billion nerve cells recording and cataloging all you hear, see, smell, taste, and touch. Your skin has more than 2 million tiny little sweat glands—about 3,000 per square inch—all a part of the intricate system that keeps your body at an even 98.6 degrees in winter or summer. You have a living pump in your chest about the size of your fist, through which your blood is pumped while traveling approximately 168 million miles a day or the equivalent of 6,720 times around the earth! The lining of your stomach contains more than 35 million glands, which aid in the process of digesting all that Mexican food you insist on eating. In one 24-hour period you breathe in more than 23,040 times as you fill your lungs with 438 cubic feet of air.
>
> On an average day you will consume about 3.5 pounds of food, drink 2.9 quarts of liquid, and lose 0.88 pound of waste. In one day's activity you will speak more than 4,800 words, move about 750 muscles, and exercise 7 million brain cells. Your body has the power to repair and rejuvenate itself as it fights off disease and infection. And these are but a few wonders operating every day, every hour, and every second of your life.[1]

You might be the only person you know who has confidence in your inner and outer beauty, because it is a totally radical way of thinking. There aren't too many people who believe they are beautiful just the way they are. It's a new way of thinking.

MAKING INNER DECISIONS TO TRUST GOD

It all comes down to the decisions you make. These inner decisions will change the course of your life. In the second chapter you looked at the part of your body you liked the least. Were you surprised to discover how the words that were spoken to you about your body kept you trapped in a poor body image?

Just as those words took such a hold on your life, so will speaking and thinking truth totally transform you. Learn to speak the truth to yourself. All these weeks you have been uncovering the truth. You've been looking into the Bible to get a biblical perspective of your body. Now it's time for you to make some decisions about how you want to show the world you are beautiful. Make some decisions about your body, your sexuality, how you care for your body, and what you believe about guys.

About Your Body

Can you say, "I praise You, God, because I am fearfully and wonderfully made" and really mean it? How are you fearfully and wonderfully made? What is most incredible to you about your body? What amazes you about God when you think of the way He formed you?

Make a commitment to be more thoughtful about the words you speak about your body. It's not easy to do, even when you've written a book on the subject. Watch yourself when you are with a group of girls. Don't join in the body bashing. Try to change the subject to talk about each other's character or positive body features. Especially watch your inner self-talk when you are looking in the mirror or trying on bathing suits. These thoughts and conversations do make an impact on how you live.

About Sexuality

Do you accept that you are a sexual being and that it is a good thing to be created as a sexual being? Do you understand that Satan wants to use your sexuality against you to separate you from God and cause you harm? Do you believe that God loves you and would never tell you to do something that would be bad for you?

We hope that you will make some major decisions about your body and how you will be different from your culture in determining what is right for you sexually. We hope that you will think about what sexual behaviors you will participate in before marriage. If you have already blown it sexually, ask God for forgiveness and make decisions about how to avoid that kind of behavior in the future.

About Caring for Your Body

Have you decided how you will care for your body without becoming obsessed with diet and exercise? What decisions are right for you? Do you have general guidelines for diet, activity, rest, work, and so on that will keep you healthy?

About Guys and Your Body

What will you do about the guys in your life and their view of your body? We hope you will make some important inner decisions not to let a boy's opinion of your looks change how you see yourself.

I (Debi) wish I could go on a campaign to teach boys not to talk negatively about girls' bodies. I honestly don't think guys, or fathers for that matter, have any idea what impact their words have on girls and women. The sad reality is that criticizing girls' bodies has a negative impact on boys and men as well.

I wish I could teach guys that if they do not overfocus on what girls look like, they will set themselves up for a lifetime of very satisfying sexual experiences within marriage. It's so true. Guys naturally focus on girls' bodies, but it will serve them well to learn how to control their thoughts and their exposure to sexually explicit material. When men (or women) focus only on the intensity of sexual experiences they can develop sexual additions that lead to unsatisfying sex and dangerous or even life-threatening sex. Sex in marriage is God's best. Any counterfeit from Satan has lots of destructive consequences.

Guys don't get fashion. We interviewed a group of boys in spring 2006 when the baby doll top was the newest trend. One boy told us he got in a lot of trouble for commenting that a certain girl looked fat in that top. He was just being honest.

The guys told us that when a girl asks them, "Do I look fat?" she is feeling insecure and is just searching for a compliment. They also said that when girls are worrying about their looks, it gets annoying. The girl should know a guy either likes her or he doesn't, and changing her makeup or hairstyle won't help. Guys don't care to hear about your body woes. Also, if a girl is wearing revealing clothes, it tells a guy she wants male attention. The group had no doubts about that.

Healing Others through Affirmation

Every day the female soul is assailed by tormenting rebukes about her unsightly body flaws. This inhumane treatment shows no signs of decline in magazines, the entertainment industry, or advertising. It's time for girls to gather together and fight against the message of despair. It's a new day, and one by one and together we can make a difference. We can affirm one another with words of hope, the Word of God. We can change the brutal reality we all live with.

Once you have tasted the goodness of God and accepted the beauty He made inside you, you will have the privilege of offering this same kind of healing to others. We live in a world plagued by broken dreams and airbrushed facades. However, there is a dream of beauty that is possible and attainable for every girl. That is the dream of being loved just the way you are. It is to be affirmed and embraced right now, this moment. Every girl is released from the fear that she is unwanted when she entrusts her heart to the loving arms of God.

Have you found the reality of your dream to be loved and beautiful just as you are? In the musical version of *Man of La Mancha*, Aldonza is a peasant whore who is not considered very attractive. Don Quixote (who thinks he is a knight killing dragons that are actually windmills) calls her his lady, his Dulcinea (which means "utter sweetness" in Spanish). Every time he sees her, he treats her as his true love, the ultimate lady.

When Don Quixote is on his deathbed, he once again calls her his Dulcinea. She responds by revealing her abusive childhood and subsequent vocation as a "kitchen slut." In spite of this, Don Quixote says, "Never deny thou art Dulcinea."

The next time she sees him, he has had a sudden burst of reality, and he tells her he doesn't know her. She kneels beside him and calls him her lord. She reminds him that he called her Dulcinea. They dream together for a moment before Don Quixote dies.

Afterward Sancho, Quixote's trusted squire, addresses her by her name, Aldonza. She responds, "My name is Dulcinea."[2] She no longer sees herself as a whore. She now sees what is utterly beautiful about her. It may seem an impossible dream, but it's not. We've lived it. You can live it too.

Are you that girl? Will you join us in sharing the good news? Perhaps we'll start a trend that will last. The world definitely needs it.

Rachel: I pray that God has spoken to you through this experience. I am in this battle with you. There is rarely a day I wake up and don't face the temptation to think negatively about myself. However, I have to renew my mind with God's truth! I'm praying we all will stand strong against our culture's lies. I am with you!

Debi: This book was an assignment from God that began many years ago. I'm not sure what will result from writing it, but my prayer is that it will change the hearts of girls so they will not doubt their beauty and will be available to find their real purpose in this world. I hope to meet you someday and see the beauty God put together to uniquely form you.

If I never see you on this earth, I can't wait to see your new body in heaven and rejoice with you in our Creator for all the goodness He has put into making you you and me me. I praise God because we are both fearfully (reverently, in complete awe, stunned into silence) and wonderfully made!

Weekly Challenge

Look up each scripture you read this week that gives God's perspectives on the human body. Then, write a letter to your body confirming the decision you have made about your body and who you really are.

Just between Girls

1. How have the girls in the group helped you the most and why?
2. What do you find most attractive about your friends here?
3. What do you find most attractive about yourself?
4. How do you hope you will look on the outside 10 years from now?
5. How do you hope you will feel about how you look 10 years from now?
6. What steps can you take to start a new trend toward body acceptance?
7. How does God's Word affirm your beauty?

Help for Those with Deeper Issues

This study may have made you realize just how much a poor body image has affected your life. As you have probably noticed, it's rare to find anyone who doesn't think that something is unattractive about her body. This is a common problem.

Of course, not everyone has developed addictions and destructive behaviors due to a poor body image, but don't feel discouraged if you have. Some problems associated with poor body image need more help and attention than this book and a study group can provide. Get help for yourself and those you love. Talk to your leader and your parents about the concerns you recognize in your life. Though these are deeper problems, they are not unsolvable.

EATING DISORDERS

Compulsive Overeating

Women who find themselves addicted to food feel that they are moral failures. They believe that if they had more self-discipline, this problem would instantly go away. They are ashamed to get help and many times don't feel that they deserve help. Help is available.

Maybe you feel that you've tried everything and there is just something different about you. That is not true. Jeremiah 29:11-14 promises that God has a plan for you and that you will find it when you search for Him with all your heart. God does want you to learn how to turn your addiction to food into dependence on Him. Women have overcome their addiction to food in a variety of ways. It is not the tool (Weight Watchers, First Place, for example); it is the relationship with God that makes the biggest difference. Don't give up! Seek guidance and counsel.

Confess your desire to stop your addiction to a spiritual person who can give you support and a professional who can help you unlock the door to your food addiction. Doing this body-image Bible study is a great foundation for overcoming the dependence you have on food. I hope you have come to accept your body a little more through the things you have written, what you have read, and the love and acceptance you have experienced from your group and from God.

Do not seek help with an eating plan to lose weight! Do seek help with an eating plan to take care of your body. Eat healthfully out of gratefulness and appreciation for the gift of your body. Do it to take care of yourself, not to make yourself look better on the outside. It is good to have a bottom-line weight that you won't go under, but don't have a goal weight that says, "I am suitable to present to the world since I weigh this now!" In fact, it would be great if you threw out the scales and evaluated the results of your eating plan by how you feel (the energy you have) and how your clothes fit.

Anorexia/Bulimia

Just as in the case of compulsive overeating, anorexia (compulsive restricting) and bulimia (compulsive eating along with purging the food with laxatives, throwing up, compulsive exercising, or a combination of these) are addictive behaviors. You need the help of someone, a professional or a group, to stop these life-threatening and destructive behaviors.

There are many facets to this problem. A negative body image is just one aspect. Food and eating habits are not the problem; they are the symptoms. You need to learn how to understand and accept yourself in order to stop the self-destructive behavior. Talk to your leader and your parents about any of these symptoms you recognize in your life. Signs that you might have an eating disorder:

- You are underweight for your age, height, and build.
- You have eating rituals—either how much you eat, what you eat, or when you eat.
- You exercise more than an hour on three to four days a week.
- You throw up your food.
- You restrict your eating.
- You have stopped menstruating.

Body Dysmorphic Disorder

This is a real and growing problem. It is characterized by delusional obsessions with imagined or slight physical imperfections. It can drive women to depression, suicide, or isolation from others. Experts believe that it is underdiagnosed. If you suspect that you are over-reacting to physical characteristics, you should seek professional help.

Cutting

Physically cutting or hurting yourself is an issue that can become compulsive. If you have done this, you should tell someone and talk about why you did it. Seek professional help to uncover how this behavior has become your way of dealing with stress and other feelings in your life.

Cosmetic Surgery

There are appropriate reasons to have plastic surgery. It's wonderful that there are so many skilled physicians God can use in the healing process. Before you have plastic surgery, think about it, talk to people you respect who can give you sound, healthy advice, and consider the options available to you. You should include among your advisors your parents, your primary care physician, and your counselor. It is not a sin to have plastic surgery, but it is important for you to think through this decision and recognize what your motivation and goals really are.

Most procedures require anesthesia. You need to fully understand the risks and consider whether they are worth taking in your particular case. In the majority of situations, cosmetic surgery is not worth the risk and money required.

Depression

Depression is characterized by a change in sleep patterns, change in appetite, overwhelming feelings of worthlessness, lack of concentration, lack of motivation, loss of energy, agitation, restlessness, irritability, or thoughts of death or suicide. It is important that you recognize the symptoms of depression and seek help. It can be treated.

There are many causes of depression. It is possible to develop depression from constantly berating yourself and your body. If you have the symptoms listed above, please discuss them with your parents, your family doctor, or a Christian counselor.

ANXIETY

Anxiety is characterized by intense worry, nervousness, panic attacks, and overwhelming fear of situations and circumstances. It can often lead to fear of leaving your home. As with depression, anxiety can be treated. You can overcome panic and fear with the help of God, your doctor, and a Christian counselor.

Focus on the Family has counselors available between 9 A.M. and 4:30 P.M. mountain time. If you would like to speak to a counselor or be referred to a counselor in your area, call 1-800-A-FAM-ILY (1-800-232-6459). Please be patient if a counselor is not immediately available. Someone will return your call.

How to Help a Friend or Loved One

Helping Someone with an Eating Disorder

When you suspect someone you love has an eating disorder, you want to do something. God can use you to help that person get help. Often your natural instincts are to persuade the individual to eat more food. A common reaction is to even try to force the person to eat. This does little good. Here is a list of dos and don'ts.

Don't
- get into power struggles over food
- offer pat answers
- impose guilt
- take responsibility for the person

Do
- lovingly be honest about the symptoms you see and your concerns
- encourage the person to get help
- encourage her to take responsibility for herself
- talk openly and honestly about your feelings
- give honest feedback about appearance
- recognize that the problem isn't just food
- listen
- show love and affection

How to Lead a Beauty Secrets Group

If you've led other groups, you'll find that this one is similar, but there will be some special issues to be aware of. First, remember that body image is a painful issue for some teen girls. Many have been deeply wounded by the comments of friends, family members, and even strangers. It is, therefore, extremely important that the teens in your group feel a sense of safety and acceptance. No one should feel put down. As the leader, you will need to address any inappropriate comments so that spirits aren't wounded further. Make it a ground rule in the first meeting that no one will criticize another's appearance.

The questions within each chapter would be most beneficial if the girls answered them in their own journals. Since there isn't space in the book to write their answers, we suggest that they buy a notebook or journal in which they can keep their personal answers. They do not have to share anything from their journals in group time, but they may want to bring them to the meetings to make notes or to refer to if they do want to share from them.

GROUND RULES

Following are ground rules for a successful group discussion. Your group may have additional suggestions.

1. Everything said here is confidential.

2. Everything said here is voluntary. You may pass if you don't want to give an answer.

3. There are no right answers. (Most answers aren't right or wrong; rather, they reflect your feelings or opinions. However, the Bible is the supreme authority.)

Your group may want to add other guidelines, but these have proven helpful in making girls feel comfortable about what they share.

At your first meeting, explain that there will be a few times when they will be asked to share information with the group, but answering questions will always be voluntary. Many shy girls might be intimidated by group sharing. In the first meeting, however, most should be able to share at least a little basic information about themselves. Begin by having them share where they go to school, how they heard about this group, if they have a pet, and so on. Keep it light and short—nothing too personal.

The discussion questions at the end of each chapter will be the focus of the sharing time; however, your group might sometimes wish to discuss questions from the text as well. Assume that each participant read the chapter during the previous week. There's really no need for formal teaching; merely discuss what was read.

Above all, I hope that the study group will provide you with a sense of community. Girls need to have deep connections with each other and with mentors. The community becomes a place where the transformation from body loathing to body acceptance can take place. Richard Foster gave this advice for a small group he led:

Give encouragement as often as possible;
advice, once in a great while;

reproof, only when absolutely necessary;
and judgment never.[1]

That's a good credo to use in your group. The goal of the group is to support one another in the process of allowing God to transform your lives and beliefs about who you are.

SUGGESTIONS FOR PRAYER

I encourage young women to have some kind of prayer list during group Bible studies like this. A bond of intimacy develops as you pray for one another. I encourage you to close each discussion time in prayer. This eliminates the problem of taking too much time sharing details of prayer requests at the beginning, which leaves the group without enough time for study.

Another way to cover prayer requests is to provide a sheet where each person can write hers before the session. If you have access to a copier during the study, you could make enough copies for everyone to take home for personal prayer. Another idea is to use e-mail to share requests with one another.

LEADING THE GROUP

I have included discussion questions at the end of each chapter. You need to decide how you will use these in your group time. If you have a very talkative group, you may not be able to use all the questions. Choose three or four that you think are most helpful from the study that week, then do the remainder if time permits.

You may want to write some of your own discussion questions.

Some leaders will give a brief overview of the chapter before going into the discussion questions. Make sure that you spend time preparing your heart and listening to God tell you how He wants you to lead.

You don't have to teach this material. Everyone has read the chapter, so if you do not feel gifted at teaching, don't try to teach. If you have a gift for teaching and feel it would be helpful to the girls, share your insights before discussion.

I hope that you will see yourself as a facilitator. You are there to encourage discussion and learning. You can set the example by sharing first so others will follow, but don't do this every time.

Don't be afraid of silence. The biggest mistake leaders make is to be intimidated by silence. It doesn't mean that no one is getting anything out of the study. If you don't experience times of silence, some will never share. If you are particularly worried about silence, try counting slowly (and silently) to 10 before jumping in to share or moving on to the next question. Trust that God is at work in the silence.

Be sensitive to the personalities in your group. If you have someone who is shy, she will need extra encouragement from you as she shares. If you have someone who is taking over the group, be sensitive to the others by making sure the group is helpful to everyone. You shouldn't be bashful about interrupting and redirecting the group if it is going in the wrong direction or if someone is dominating the discussion. Most of the questions don't have right or wrong answers, but if anyone is sharing heresy or untruths about God's Word, you should gently but firmly confront her.

Your life will be touched as much as the lives of the girls you lead through this experience. I pray that you will enjoy seeing how God works through you.

Notes

Chapter 1

1. Margo Maine, *Body Wars: An Activist's Guide* (Carlsbad, CA: Gurze Books, 2000), 78.
2. "Eating Disorder Awareness Week—Some Scary Stats," www.kidzworld.com/site/p3155.htm
3. Denise Lavoie, "Librarian Sues Harvard Over 'Pretty' Bias," The Associated Press, http://Abcnews.go.com/Technology/ print?id=603158
4. Marielena Palma, "Perk Up Your Chest!" http://www.ediets .com/news/pringArticle.cfm?ccid=7&cmi=2115493
5. ABC News, *20/20* Transcript #1539;5.
6. Located at http://www.christianity.co.nz/esteem4.htm.

Chapter 2

1. Bethany Dillon, *Bethany Dillon*, "Beautiful," Sparrow Records, 2004. Used by permission.

Chapter 3

1. Katherine McPhee, "My Secret Struggle," *People* magazine, Vol. 66, no. 1, July 3, 2006.

Chapter 4

1. *The Oprah Winfrey Show*, Harpo Productions, April 24, 2006; 12.

2. Debra Evans, *Beauty and the Best* (Colorado Springs, CO: Focus on the Family, 1993), 106-7.
3. Locks of Love, www.locksoflove.org, 2925 10th Avenue North, Suite 102, Lake Worth, FL 33461, Phone: (561) 963-1677, Toll Free: (888) 896-1588

Chapter 5
1. J. Utter, D. Neumark-Sztainer, M. Wall, et al.: "Reading magazine articles about dieting and associated weight control behaviors among adolescents," *Journal of Adolescent Health*, 2003; 32: 78-82.
2. American Academy of Dermatology, www.aad.org.

Chapter 6
1. David Foster, *Accept No Mediocre Life* (New York: Warner Faith, 2005), 100-101.

2. *Man of La Mancha*, United Artists, 1972.

Appendix 3
1. Richard Foster, as quoted by James Bryan Smith and Lynda Graybeal, *A Spiritual Formation Workbook* (San Francisco: HarperCollins, 1993), 9.

FOCUS ON THE FAMILY®

Welcome to the family!

Whether you purchased this book, borrowed it, or received it as a gift, we're glad you're reading it. It's just one of the many helpful, encouraging, and biblically based resources produced by Focus on the Family for people in all stages of life.

Focus began in 1977 with the vision of one man, Dr. James Dobson, a licensed psychologist and author of numerous best-selling books on marriage, parenting, and family. Alarmed by the societal, political, and economic pressures that were threatening the existence of the American family, Dr. Dobson founded Focus on the Family with one employee and a once-a-week radio broadcast aired on 36 stations.

Now an international organization reaching millions of people daily, Focus on the Family is dedicated to preserving values and strengthening and encouraging families through the life-changing message of Jesus Christ.

Focus on the Family Magazines

These faith-building, character-developing publications address the interests, issues, concerns, and challenges faced by every member of your family from preschool through the senior years.

| Focus on the Family **Citizen®** U.S. news issues | Focus on the Family **Clubhouse Jr.™** Ages 4 to 8 | Focus on the Family **Clubhouse™** Ages 8 to 12 | **Breakaway®** Teen guys | **Brio®** Teen girls 12 to 16 | **Brio & Beyond®** Teen girls 16 to 19 | **Plugged In®** Reviews movies, music, TV |

FOR MORE INFORMATION

 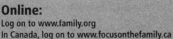

Online:
Log on to www.family.org
In Canada, log on to www.focusonthefamily.ca

Phone:
Call toll free: (800) A-FAMILY (232-6459)
In Canada, call toll free: (800) 661-9800

More Great Resources
from Focus on the Family®

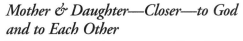

Mother & Daughter—Closer—to God and to Each Other

Take one part talking, two parts listening, sprinkle liberally with Scripture and fun activities, and what do you have? Susie Shellenberger's book *Closer*, written especially for mothers and teen daughters to experience together.

Want More? Joy
By Jeanette Hanscome

Teen girls wrestle with life's tough questions while juggling school, activities and relationships with parents, friends, and boys. They need assurance that God wants them to have more—more joy, more trust, more connection with Him.

Dare 2 Share: A Field Guide to Sharing Your Faith

Sharing the gospel is the most important thing you'll ever do—and, probably one of the most challenging. So, how do you do it and where do you begin? In *Dare 2 Share*, author and speaker Greg Stier equips you with a witnessing game plan and the information, support, and confidence you need to change your world for Christ.

FOR MORE INFORMATION

 Online:
Log on to www.family.org
In Canada, log on to www.focusonthefamily.ca.

 Phone:
Call toll free: (800) A-FAMILY
In Canada, call toll free: (800) 661-9800.

BP06XP1